# The Sex Trade, Evil, and Christian Theology

# The Sex Trade, Evil, and Christian Theology

GLENN M. HARDEN

With a Foreword by
Dawn Herzog Jewell

WIPF & STOCK · Eugene, Oregon

THE SEX TRADE, EVIL, AND CHRISTIAN THEOLOGY



Wipf & Stock
An Imprint of Wipf and Stock Publishers
199 W. 8th Ave., Suite 3
Eugene, OR 97401

www.wipfandstock.com

PAPERBACK ISBN 13: 978-1-4982-2383-6
HARDCOVER ISBN 13: 978-1-4982-2385-0

Manufactured in the U.S.A. 03/02/2016

To Leslie

# Contents

# Foreword

All that is necessary for the triumph of evil is
that good men do nothing.

– ATTRIBUTED TO EDMUND BURKE

I THANK GOD FOR the good men and women doing something to tackle the evil sale of human bodies for sex that's rampant in our world. The horrors of young boys and girls sold for dollars a day compels thoughtful people to "do something" and to help "rescue" them. But we are fools to enter into this mission without a better understanding of the evil that contributes to the exploitation of human flesh.

Glenn Harden offers us this thoughtful examination, allowing us to journey with him. He explores both the evil nature of the trade and insightfully considers opposing viewpoints of those who deny the evil and prefer to legalize prostitution. Ignoring the role of both God and evil does little to further the help and healing of men, women, and children who are trapped and drowning in despair around the world.

When I was researching ministries around the world fighting trafficking and commercial sexual exploitation, I quickly learned from leaders and volunteers that any effective work was marinated in many prayers beforehand. Before going on my first outreach to brothels in Athens, I participated in an almost mandatory worship time. Why? Because facing the darkness and maintaining hope requires soaking in God's holy and loving presence.

The evil in the sex trade is not overwhelming when juxtaposed with the hope that the Christian gospel offers to us and to survivors of the sex trade. But as Glenn warns us aptly, "Our participation in the Christian mission to prostitutes must be grounded in a self-understanding that acknowledges our commonality with prostitutes. We are all being rescued—if anyone is the rescuer, it is God, not us. Do we not all fall? Do we not all feel shame? See, the church is a church of prostitutes. We all need it to be a place of mercy, and that is why we must never forsake the mission to prostitutes."

May this book draw you closer to the One who rescues, and compel you to participate in loving men, women, and children outside your comfort zone.

—Dawn Herzog Jewell,
author of *Escaping the Devil's Bedroom: Sex-Trafficking, Global Prostitution and the Gospel's Transforming Power* (Monarch, 2008)

# Introduction

As theologian Kenneth Surin recognized, all discussions of evil are historically situated, and my work is no different.[1] I write as an American man living in the Dominican Republic where I have engaged in very modest efforts to help victims and survivors of the sex trade. This essay is the fruit of my reflections on the intersections of the sex trade, evil, and Christian theology.

I am not primarily interested in the "problem of evil" as posed by David Hume and J. L. Mackie, which seeks to show the logical absurdity of believing in both the existence of evil and an omnipotent and benevolent God.[2] In contrast to Mackie, but in accord with historian of philosophy Susan Neiman, I do not believe evil is a "problem" only for the theist.[3] Rather, as Neiman wrote, "the problem of evil . . . is fundamentally a problem about the intelligibility of the world as a whole."[4] While the atheist may be able to score points against the theist by framing the problem as a specific kind of logical puzzle, evil still comes back to haunt the atheist, ultimately challenging that worldview as well. As I hope to show, I do not believe that the philosophical atheist has the resources both to take evil seriously and to ground hope that lives defeated by evil can be made whole again. Like the theologian William J. Abraham,

1. Surin, *Theology and the Problem of Evil*, 9.

2. Hume, "Evil and the God of Religion," 44; Mackie, "Evil and Omnipotence," 89–90.

3. Mackie, "Evil and Omnipotence," 89.

4. Neiman, *Evil in Modern Thought*, 7–8.

who as a young atheist was attracted to Christianity because it took evil with utmost seriousness without falling into despair, I believe that Christianity offers us more hope to sustain efforts to relieve suffering and oppose evil than any of its alternatives.[5] In fact, in Christ we are offered salvation precisely because evil is so devastating and ever-present.

My argument is essentially this: the defining characteristic of evil is its *de-meaning* quality. In chapter 1, I reflect on the experience of women in the sex trade, showing how evil is inherently insensible, how it constricts freedom, how it is comprised of systems of de-meaning as well as of personal choices, and how it is personally felt as guilt and shame. I also argue that only an eternal, personal God can ensure the meaning we long for and ensure victory over evil.

In chapter 2, by reflecting on Job and the work of Christ on the cross, I explore how evil as de-meaning complicates theodicy. The Christian gospel proclaims that *lives* can be redeemed and made meaningful again in defiance of even the most horrendous evil. But because the nature of evil is de-meaning, God is not always free to act toward us as justice demands. Yet even when we face the injustice of God, we may have faith that God loves us and is at work defeating the de-meaning power of evil.

In chapter 3, I will take on the atheistic argument from evil. I will show that when evil is understood as de-meaning, it is not inconsistent for a believer to have hope. However, an atheist must either deny evil or hope in order to remain logically consistent. Given actual evidence of healing in the face of horrendous evil, I propose that atheism has a "problem of healing" that cannot be adequately explained without appealing to a personal and loving God.

In chapter 4, I will examine the feminist theology of evil of Rita Nakashima Brock and Rebecca Ann Parker. I will argue that their conflation of evil with patriarchy and their determination to approach theology from the perspective of a victim of abuse actually diminishes the resources of Christianity to help real victims of

5. Abraham, "Faraway Fields Are Green," 166.

abuse. Their proposal that true healing power comes from human interrelatedness and not from God is not a sufficient foundation to ground the healing of the world.

Finally, in chapter 5, I will examine a competing narrative of salvation that seeks to redefine prostitution as sex work and normalize it in society. I will argue that, while this approach offers important criticisms for the Christian and feminist missions to prostitutes, it ultimately fails to save women, men, and children because prostitution should properly be understood as inherently de-meaning. I will conclude by highlighting a few aspects of the Christian salvation story that are crucial for the Christian mission to prostitutes. The Christian gospel is our best hope against evil; other salvation narratives lack the resources necessary either to take evil seriously or to ground hope in defiance of evil.

Much has been written about the sex trade recently, especially human trafficking, which today is understood as a form of modern slavery. Globalization has made human trafficking relatively easy and lucrative, and the moral outrage against it seems to me to be a fundamentally healthy response. Nonetheless, we must recognize certain dangers in reading about another person's suffering, especially suffering so closely related to disreputable sex. Students of the sex trade are vulnerable to a kind of voyeurism or fascination with the sex trade that does its victims and survivors no service. In fact, it can become another objectification and commodification of people that de-means and dehumanizes them. Let the reader beware.

Some time ago, I realized that I could not continue to study the sex trade; I had to *do* something about it. To *know* but not *act* is a sort of betrayal of real people. This thesis is my corresponding reflection on my journey. As the theologian Helmut Thielicke wrote, "Essentially, theological method is characterized by the fact that it takes into account that God has spoken, and that now what God has spoken is to be understood and answered. But it can only be understood when I (1) recognize that what has been said is directed to *me*, and (2) become involved in formulating a reply."[6]

6. Thielicke, *A Little Exercise*, 34.

For some reason I do not quite understand God has spoken to me about his love for the victims and survivors of the sex trade. I can hardly open the Scriptures without being reminded of God's great concern for justice and mercy for these marginalized, broken, and oppressed people. Please understand that this work is my "hesitant, stammering" response to God's voice in my life.[7] In this sense, it is God who is my primary dialogue partner, and this work is a prayer.[8]

7. Surin, *Theology and the Problem of Evil*, 143.

8. Thielicke, *A Little Exercise*, 33–34.

# I

# The Sex Trade and the Nature of Evil

When my friend Leslie was five years old, her father abandoned her family. He handed her a note and told her to give it to her mother, saying that he would be back in a few minutes. She had loved her father with all of her heart—he was less serious than her mother and more emotionally connected to her. He did not come back. Looking back on this experience as an adult, she wrote: "I gave the letter to my mom, but my dad didn't return. I spent the rest of my childhood waiting for him to come back, and I can think of nothing crueler than to be left with the false promise of, 'I will return in a moment.' In one blow my faith in people was destroyed, and I became a sad, scared girl. I sealed up my broken heart from the pain—and from love."[1]

Her mother was devastated—in a way, Leslie lost her that day too. Her little sister looked to Leslie for guidance, but Leslie could not carry the burden of being a mother at that tender age. Her childhood was filled with a lingering sadness.

One bright spot in her life was school, which she attended at a monastery. Slowly, a measure of peace began to return to her life. She wrote:

1. Leslie Harley, email to author, 9 August 2010.

As it turned out, I loved the primary school (and later the secondary school). The nuns were very good to me, and I was obedient. I had very intense spiritual life, and the nuns contributed much to my spiritual formation. Although they taught me a mistaken way of salvation by works instead of faith, my pure heart was becoming nearer to God.

One precious day at the school that I will always remember came when I was 12. As I prayed alone in the Chapel of the Monastery, God whispered into my ear with much affection, "Come and follow me." I knew at that moment that my heart was going to have only one love the rest of its life: Jesus.

However, I was so young and timid that I kept this secret hidden in my heart like a valuable treasure. I was nervous whenever I heard the voice of Jesus, and I did not know how to communicate to others the sweet truth of what was happening. I began to listen to an inner music as I lived in communion with the new Lord of my heart.

I went for much of the year without telling anyone about my secret joy. However, my life had changed and that secret happiness started to become obvious for others to see. One day the principal of the school, a very sweet and wise nun, asked me: "Leslie, do you have something to tell me?"

Upon hearing her question, I was certain the moment had come for me to share my secret with another person. So I answered her with a broken and shy voice, "Jesus has called me."

To my surprise, she answered, "I already knew that. My question is: 'What are you going to do?'"

I simply answered, "Follow Him."

I cherished my time in the monastery. I loved everything about it: the silence, the order and the cleaning, my times alone praying to God, my friends, and the counsel I received from my spiritual advisor, the Masterful Sister of the Nuns. Those years passed seemingly without problems.[2]

2. Ibid.

Then, when she was fourteen, her father returned. He had lived in the United States and fought in Vietnam; he was no longer the same man. The longed-for reunion became a curse. He raped her.

Crushed, broken-hearted, filled with fear, anger, guilt, and pain, Leslie kept the abuse a secret and hoped to escape the world in the monastery. But her father left again and her parents' impending divorce meant that, when it came time to graduate, the authorities at the monastery would not let her profess to become a nun, believing that daughters of divorce were not suitable for the convent.

Betrayed by her father and the church, which felt like rejection by God, Leslie became an atheist and communist. She went to university to try to find some meaning in her life. She earned her degree and became a professional.

For a while she had a boyfriend, Fernando, who asked her to perform erotic fantasies for him. Broken emotionally, she was dependent upon this man, and so she would comply. One day, he asked her to prostitute herself. He took her to a bar and dropped her off. She had no idea how to prostitute herself, what to charge, or how to act. While Fernando watched from another part of the bar, an American asked her if she would accompany him to his hotel room. She wrote, "[E]verything happened so fast, now I think it was like a dream."[3] Afterwards, Fernando and she celebrated by spending the $100 she earned on drugs and alcohol.

Thus began her eleven-year career in prostitution. She described this time, thus: "For 11 years I played Russian roulette with unknown men, with alcohol, drug doses unlimited in lonely places, dangerous scenarios with sexual deviants, [with] violent men, with very competitive and vengeful prostitutes, with unscrupulous managers of bars [and] in the midst of dangerous diseases like AIDS. On two occasions, someone threatened me with a gun. [Once,] I was about to die strangled, [and I] survived two overdoses."[4]

3. Leslie Harley, email to author, 5 August 2010.

4. Ibid.

She despised Christians: they were good; she was bad. She did not want help. She denied God and, especially at first, she believed that the life was grand—she had money; she could buy what she wanted.

But, over time, the pain deepened. In moments of solitude and silence, she was deeply unhappy. She hoped that a man would come into her life and rescue her, but none came. Sometimes in the brothel, filled with sadness and watching her life evaporate, she would say a secret prayer. But more and more she began to think about her own death, until finally she resolved to take her own life.

In her book, *Horrendous Evils and the Goodness of God*, Marilyn McCord Adams is concerned with the worst sorts of evils, those she called "horrendous evils." She defined these as "evils the participation in which (that is, the doing or suffering of which) constitutes prima facie reason to doubt whether the participant's life could (given their inclusion in it) be a great good to him/her on the whole."[5] Examples of horrendous evil include "the rape of a woman and axing off her arms, psycho-physical torture whose ultimate goal is the disintegration of personality, betrayal of one's deepest loyalties, child abuse of the sort described by Ivan Karamazov, child pornography, parental incest, slow death by starvation, the explosion of nuclear bombs over populated areas."[6]

What makes this sort of evil horrendous is that it engulfs "any positive value in the participant's life" and its "destructive power reaches . . . into the deep structure of the person's frameworks of meaning-making, seemingly to defeat the individual's value as a person, to degrade him/her to subhuman status."[7]

I propose that the harm that Leslie experienced at the hands of her father and in the sex trade properly falls under Adams's definition of a "horrendous evil." The resolution to take her own life demonstrates that she no longer considered her own life a great

5. Adams, *Horrendous Evils*, 26.

6. Ibid.

7. Ibid., 26–27.

good to her. Like all prostitutes, she certainly was devalued, degraded, and treated as a thing.[8]

Using Adams's definition of evil and Leslie's (and others') experiences as a starting point, I want to consider more deeply the *character* of evil. What, exactly, is evil? Many, both atheists and Christians, have understood the problem of evil to be primarily a problem of *suffering*, especially physical suffering. C. S. Lewis's *The Problem of Pain* is an accessible Christian treatment of the problem of evil from this perspective. But in fact, the problem of evil is not a problem with suffering *per se*, but with *meaningless* suffering. And this is to say that the problem of evil is really a problem of meaning—the intelligibility of the universe, as Susan Neiman wrote.[9]

Consider William Rowe's famous example of the fawn that dies a lingering and agonizing death after a forest fire. If, according to Rowe, the deer's suffering is "pointless," then God cannot exist because a benevolent God would not permit pointless suffering.[10] Most Christian philosophers have accepted the premise that if an omniscient, benevolent God exists, pointless suffering cannot. All suffering must be meaningful.[11]

I believe that this premise should be rejected because evil is essentially pointless. I propose that evil is, in essence, *de-meaning*. We might say that evil is the privation of a special kind of good—the basic good of meaning or significance. The idea of evil as nothing is not new: Plotinus, Augustine, and Aquinas have all understood evil as a corruption or absence of good.[12] But I want to draw attention to evil's de-meaning quality. Much pain and suffering *is* meaningful, and in this way, does not pose a threat to a person's valuing of their own life. The pain of childbirth, for

8. See also Jeffreys, "Prostitution as a Harmful Cultural Practice," 389–92.

9. Neiman, *Evil in Modern Thought*, 7–8.

10. See Rowe, "The Problem of Evil" and "Friendly Atheism."

11. Wykstra, "The Humean Obstacle"; Alston, "The Inductive Argument from Evil"; Swinburne, *Providence and the Problem of Evil*. See Hasker's helpful discussion of this debate in his *The Triumph of God over Evil*, 177–87.

12. Plotinus, *The Enneads* 1.8.3; Augustine, *Confessions* 7.18–19; Thomas Aquinas, *Summa Theologica* 1.49.1.

example, is overwhelmed by the goodness of bringing a new life into the world. Moreover, significant amounts of evil can be incorporated into a meaningful life; consider how many people who have experienced abuse or pain go on to help others with similar problems. Nonetheless, some evil does undermine the meaning in one's life, and horrendous evil, as Adams wrote, threatens the very ability to make or see meaning in one's life so that life is no longer considered a good.

What does it mean, then, to make meaning? What is *meaning*? In this essay, I am not primarily concerned with the sort of meaning that implies understanding, but with the sort of meaning that implies valuing. An event, a life, a thing, a person *means* something when it holds significance or value for a person, community, or other meaning-maker. Both the individual human and human communities are loci of meaning. That is, persons make meaning in the context of their community; they cannot make meanings alone. This is because the articulation and representation of meaning is based on language that is possessed by the community. Pre-language human infants are utterly dependent upon others so that any pre-language meaning-making must be in relation to others. Moreover, it seems that to be a genuine meaning-maker, one must possess memory; for meanings must be *held*, not simply formulated and forgotten. Meaning is more than goal-directed behavior, which humans share with non-human animals. (While beyond the scope of my study, I hold open the possibility that some of the higher non-human animals might be meaning-makers.) Rather, memory integrates meanings of life events into an intelligible whole. We humans always relate meaning through storytelling.[13]

The significance of a person is not dependent upon his or her capacity or capability as a meaning-maker. Consider this example: What is the meaning of the *Mona Lisa*? Does the *Mona Lisa* create its own meaning? Of course not; rather the meaning of the *Mona*

13. This is well understood by psychologists. See Emmons, *The Psychology of Ultimate Concerns*, 45; Singer and Salovey, *The Remembered Self*; Adler, *The Science of Living*, 108. Stump's *Wandering in Darkness* also explores the problem of evil as problem for storytelling. I use "storytelling" in a broad sense here so that music could also be included.

*Lisa* is bestowed upon it by the human community. The same principle applies to humans and animals. A human individual's meaning is not dependent upon his or her capacities—not even those capacities required to make meaning, such as linguistic ability, sociability, or memory. A person with advanced Alzheimer's disease is still *meaningful*, even if his or her capacity to make meaning has been lost or severely constrained. Similarly, the dead remain significant to the living for some time after their death. Yet, the dead can no longer be meaning-makers (unless resurrected).

Meaning is bestowed by meaning-makers but meaning is not dependent on being a meaning-maker. Those beings that possess language and memory and are in some way connected to a community are meaning-makers. Healthy, living humans fit this description and are therefore able to bestow meaning on events, people, animals, and things.

Meaning is a kind of *relation*. It is not something that exists of its own, but always *in-relation-to*. The Jewish theologian Martin Buber captured the importance of relation for living in his influential if opaque *I and Thou*. He described two "primary words": *I-Thou* and *I-It*. We experience the world through the *I-It*. The *It* is an object, "bounded by others." In contrast, the *I-Thou* is relation; when addressing a fellow human as *Thou*, that person is not experienced as an object among objects, but is encountered.[14] Or, as Buber more poetically wrote, "All real living is meeting."[15]

Most, I suspect, will agree that healthy humans make meaning, that they do this in context of communities, and that meaning is always relational. So far, so good. But in order to establish meaning, do we need more than the human community? Do we need something that is transcendent and personal in which to ground meaning? Is God necessary for meaning?

I argue that God is indeed necessary. But, in order to explain why, first we need to understand the threat that death is to meaning-making. For all that we can tell by appearances, we cease to exist at death and are therefore unable to make meaning of our

14. Buber, *I and Thou*, 3–9.

15. Ibid., 11.

lives or anything else. For it is obvious that in order to make meaning, one must be alive. Now, the death of the individual is certainly a threat to our own individual narratives, but it is not the end of meaning because communities outlive individual members. Thus, families, tribes, nations, churches, businesses, schools, and other groups will continue to remember and value the dead, at least for a time. And once a person is forgotten, a person's influence may still continue, however tenuously, through their offspring, productive labor, or ideas. So it is that most people, if not all, situate their meaning into the greater narratives told by the communities to which they belonged. Thus, we intuitively understand genocide to be a greater evil than the sum total of the individual murders of which it is comprised because genocide threatens not only individuals but the significance of all individuals associated with the community itself.

To many, community may seem sufficient as a ground for meaning, but it is still wanting. For, in fact, communities also die and cease to exist. Historically, genocide has proven effective: there simply are no longer Arawak communities in the Caribbean; they have been completely annihilated.[16] Even gradual, non-destructive change can threaten the meaning of communities, as is suggested by those who wonder if the United States of the present is what its founders fought and died to secure. But let me be even more direct: science teaches us that one day the solar system will no longer be able to support human life. Moreover, there will come a day when there will be no place in the universe that can support any kind of life.[17] Ultimately, humanity will come to an end. When that happens, all meaning held by the human community will be lost. Since I argue that memory is necessary for meaning, then we will no longer mean anything once we are gone and no one is left to remember. Extending our meaning through genetically-altered

16. Rogoziński, *A Brief History of the Caribbean*, 32.

17. See, for example, Islam, *The Ultimate Fate of the Universe*, 105–11. Islam actually argues that it will be possible for very advanced and technically ingenious civilization to exist even after super-massive galactic black holes have evaporated completely some $10^{100}$ years from now. I find this proposition dubious in the extreme.

human descendants, artificial intelligence, or friendly aliens only buys us a little extra time. Eventually they will all be gone too.

The philosopher Bertrand Russell understood this. He asked how we might "preserve [our] aspirations untarnished;" for it was clear to him that: "Man is the product of cause which had no prevision of the end they were achieving; that his origin, his growth, his hopes and fears, his loves and his beliefs, are but the outcome of accidental collocations of atoms; that no fire, no heroism, no intensity of thought and feeling, can preserve an individual life beyond the grave; that all the labours of the ages, all the devotion, all the inspiration, all the noonday brightness of human genius, are destined to extinction in the vast death of the solar system, and that the whole temple of Man's achievement must inevitably be buried beneath the debris of a universe in ruins."[18]

Russell's solution was to cherish love and resist the irresistible—not much in which to ground significance because, without an eternal community, there is no rational justification for these ethics. He continues to write with great admiration for human courage and community in the face of such sure desolation, even as he recognizes its ultimate extinction:

> Brief and powerless is Man's life; on him and all his race the slow, sure doom falls pitiless and dark. Blind to good and evil, reckless of destruction, omnipotent matter rolls on its relentless way; for Man, condemned today to lose his dearest, tomorrow himself to pass through the gate of darkness, it remains only to cherish, ere yet the blow falls, the lofty thoughts that ennoble his little day; disdaining the coward terrors of the slave of Fate, to worship at the shrine that his own hands have built; undismayed by the empire of chance, to preserve a mind free from the wanton tyranny that rules his outward life; proudly defiant of the irresistible forces that tolerate, for a moment, his knowledge and his condemnation, to sustain alone, a weary but unyielding Atlas, the world that his

18. Russell, "A Free Man's Worship," 41.

> own ideals have fashioned despite the trampling march of unconscious power.[19]

Yet in the face of that actual "unconscious power" or even human mistreatment of one's fellows, I fear that Russell's poetic phrases will be of little succor for the broken-hearted. The historian Carlos Eire said of Russell's philosophy, "Safety in despair; if that is not a leap of faith, nothing else is."[20] For in the end, we still die and will be forgotten; all memory of our heroic striving will cease; the universe will be empty of stories and so evil will be completely victorious.

Why isn't one life enough? Why do we long for transcendent, eternal meaning? That many of us do in fact long for this has been widely acknowledged by our philosophers and poets, including both those who believe in such meaning and those who do not. In describing this longing, the Spanish philosopher-poet Miguel de Unamuno declared, "Not to be all and for ever is as if not to be—at least, let me be my whole self, and be so for ever and ever."[21] Either this longing is the curse of blind evolution—a desire that we are damned always to be denied—or we really will possess eternal life. It is an old Christian truth that we are "made for eternity." C. S. Lewis argued, "If I find in myself a desire which no experience in this world can satisfy, the most probable explanation is that I was made for another world."[22]

What we need to escape the ultimate loss of meaning is a transcendent being that can hold our meaning eternally. Since meaning can only be held if one possesses sociability, community, and memory, then this transcendent meaning-maker must be personal. More specifically, the transcendent meaning-maker must be eternally and personally in community—just the sort of Trinitarian God that Christianity proclaims. What Christianity offers, then, is an eternal source of meaning.

19. Ibid., 47.

20. Eire, *A Very Brief History of Eternity*, 14.

21. Unamuno, *Tragic Sense of Life*, 39.

22. Lewis, *Mere Christianity*, 120.

But it gets better, for God not only holds meaning, but he resurrects us too so that we can all share history forever. Over time, as the Jewish theologian Jon D. Levenson has persuasively argued, the Jews worked through the tension between the universal fact of death and the promises of God to restore Israel by coming to believe in a doctrine of universal resurrection. This idea did not come to the Jews from the Persians, but developed gradually from Jewish sources that suggested God's healing power and victory *must* overcome death if God is to keep his promises.[23] Christianity announced that the first fruits of God's reign had arrived with the resurrection of Jesus Christ, the Son of God. If the Christian good news is true, then, we have hope that not only will the significance of our lives and works be preserved but also that we will share the memory of the story for eternity.

Not only are we meaning-makers but the personal, transcendent, Triune God of Christianity bestows meaning upon us by loving us and inviting us into the divine story. God is the source of *ultimate* meaning so that the meanings that we make are either found in God or are, in fact, meaningless because they are the very actions or ideas by which we de-mean ourselves or others. Meanings that deviate from God's story and cannot be reconciled to it—one thinks of the Nazi vision of German salvation—are contrary to divine reality. We could use the language of truth and falsehood—meanings that align with God's meanings are "true" while meanings that do not so align are "false." Ultimately, our acts that destroy others and the meanings of others—rape, shame, violence, genocide, etc.—are acts that will need to be overcome through healing, reconciliation, and re-meaning. One consequence of having an ultimate meaning-maker is that the meanings produced within our own human communities will face judgment and, in some cases, will be found wanting.

To summarize my argument thus far: evil should not be understood as a problem of suffering, but as a problem of meaning. Evil is inherently de-meaning and it is the loss of meaning that makes something evil. Meaning depends on language, memory,

23. Levenson, *Resurrection and the Restoration of Israel.*

and community, and only a personal, eternal God can guarantee meaning in face of the threat of death and extinction to human communities. The God of Judaism and Christianity promises to do just that, not only by loving us but also by inviting us to participate in the divine story and resurrecting us, and so God offers us a secure ground for ultimate meaning.

I want to turn to examine more closely how evil is experienced. Fundamentally, we experience evil in two overlapping ways: it can be experienced as losing one's ability to make meaning (or causing one to lose this ability), and it can be experienced when one is treated in a way contrary to one's transcendent meaning (or when one treats someone in this way). The former is another way to describe what Adams calls "horrendous evils," because someone who can no longer make sense of her life is someone whose life is no longer a great good to her. But, generally, the former cannot be experienced without the latter. That is, horrendous evil does not normally come out of the blue, but is caused by being treated contrary to one's transcendent meaning, that is, being treated as if one were not beloved by God.

Assaults on our dignity come from both human and non-human agents. The de-meaning evil that results is experienced as active, personal and a constriction of our freedom (that is, our ability to make meaning in our lives). Our participation in evil—as victim or perpetrator—also brings feelings of guilt and shame. Prostitution is a system of evil that exemplifies all of these experiences.

Before going into more depth about these points, I want to first consider an aside about non-human agents that cause de-meaning evil. Christianity teaches that death is not "natural," rather it is an enemy that God will defeat. Thus, cancer, tsunamis, and other natural destructive forces are disordered, and humans experience them as violations of their dignity, even though these events do not have personal volition of their own. But does God then cause them?

Herein we have a tension within Christianity and Judaism. For God is clearly the Lord of nature: Jesus is able to still the waters with a word.[24] Yet, creation is also "subjected to futility;" it is not what it should be.[25] By faith we believe that "this world [is] only a shadow of the fuller, richer, more substantial, more glorious creation that God intends" and that it "is a shattered mirror of divine beauty, still full of light, but riven by darkness."[26] Nature is good, yet broken; God is Lord, yet not all is under his reign. Why is this? While many theologians have interpreted the Fall described in Genesis 2 and 3 to indicate that natural evil ultimately has volitional causes from personal created agents (either angelic or human), Scripture as a whole is more nuanced.

The ninth chapter of John describes an encounter between Jesus, his disciples, and a man born blind. The chapter begins with a question about the origins of natural evil. The disciples ask Jesus, "[W]ho sinned, this man or his parents, that he was born blind?" (John 9:2). Like many Christian theologians today, they assumed that a personal agent must be responsible for the natural evil of being born blind. The response of Jesus is instructive, however, in that it cautions us against moving to such conclusions. Rather, the responsibility for evil is set in the passive voice—he simply "was born blind," but the *purpose* of this de-meaning natural evil was "so that God's works might be revealed in him" (John 9:3). Jesus does not seem especially concerned with the cause of natural evil, but, as his subsequent actions show, he is extremely concerned to show what God is doing about this evil. It is no small matter that the life of the man born blind has a purpose—that is, meaning—and that meaning is revealed through God's healing of natural evil. While this perspective is not going to satisfy every inquirer, by focusing on God's redeeming activity we may yet find hope for healing in a world that includes cancer, earthquakes, or being born blind.

Whether through non-human or human agents, evil is experienced as an active and personal force. While many Christian theologians and philosophers have argued that evil is essentially *nothing*, they have nonetheless understood it is not *felt* as nothing;

24. Matt 8:26; Mark 4:39.

25. Rom 8:20.

26. Hart, *The Doors of the Sea*, 102.

in fact, it is a powerful destructive force, and most of the time, demeaning is felt as if it is a *personal* assault on one's dignity, even if it comes through natural forces such as cancer or tsunamis.

In one of the most important modern works of theodicy (broadly defined), Augustine's modern and secular Jewish student Hannah Arendt reflected on the meaning of the trial of Adolf Eichmann for his crimes against the Jewish people and humanity during the Holocaust.[27] Here, she came to understand evil as something superficial: "Evil possesses neither depth nor any demonic dimension. It can overgrow and lay waste the whole world precisely because it spreads like a fungus on the surface."[28]

Arendt is trying to make evil both comprehensible and lend hope for its defeat.[29] By arguing that it is merely "banal," and not demonic, she understands the evil of Eichmann and the Holocaust as mere "thoughtlessness." Eichmann was no "villain," rather, "[e]xcept for an extraordinary diligence in looking out for his personal advancement, he had no motives at all. And this diligence in itself was in no way criminal; he certainly would never have murdered his superior in order to inherit his post. He *merely*, to put the matter colloquially, *never realized what he was doing.*"[30]

The Court could not abide the suspicion that Eichmann was, in fact, a "clown," for such a "suspicion would have been fatal to the whole enterprise, and was also rather hard to sustain in view of the sufferings he had caused to millions of people."[31] In considering Eichmann's complicity in evil, Arendt had revealed how evil could be meaningless for the perpetrator, yet felt as a deeply personal assault on the dignity of the victim. Evil thus has this dual characteristic: an inexplicability—a thoughtlessness and meaninglessness, but also a deeply active and powerful assault on meaning.

27. For the connection between Arendt and Augustine, see Elshtain, *Augustine and the Limits of Politics*, 69; Gregory, *Politics and the Order of Love*, 198–201.

28. Neiman, *Evil in Modern Thought*, 301, citing Arendt..

29. Neiman, *Evil in Modern Thought*, 301–4.

30. Arendt, *Eichmann in Jerusalem*, 287.

31. Ibid., 54.

While Arendt eschews the demonic as too appealing and perhaps too great to confront, no doubt many will continue to understand evil personalized in demonic forces. Arendt is trying to understand how evil came to be, but the victim is trying to understand what it means for them. The personalization of evil in demonic forces is a *story* that helps recover meaning from the abyss. It is, in fact, a way of trying to endure. In this sense, Arendt who understands evil as an undirected fungus and the victim who feels it as a demonic presence share the same goal, that of fostering hope that opposing evil will not be in vain.

The connection between belief in demonic forces and the fact that the victim feels personally assaulted by evil is not always understood by modern scholars. For example, the historian Joseph F. Kelly connects belief in Satan with the "demonization" of other people.[32] But it seems to me that the relationship works the other way. People easily understand the existential threat other people may pose to them and, thus, religion is not needed to demonize others. So when people experience the indignities of evil uncaused by human agents, they may interpret those events as personal assaults by demonic forces. Thus, a lifestory that includes personal demonic forces makes more sense to many than one that excludes it.

That evil is active and personal is how the book of Job portrays it. The Accuser (*Satan*) of Job (and of God, indirectly) actually de-means Job with his accusation. The accusation is, in a sense, a nothing—a lie, but also an assault on Job's dignity. For Job, unaware of the prompting accusation, the resulting evil that overcomes him certainly feels personal.

Evil is also felt as a trap or a constriction of liberty—which it certainly is. While no one is completely autonomous, some real freedom is necessary to make meaning of one's life. When one is forced into complying with other people's desires, one's ability to lead a life meaningful to oneself is severely constricted. When one is compelled to commit acts of evil, one's life can contradict one's envisioned and true meaning for it; one's own life may no longer

32. Kelly, *The Problem of Evil*, 110–18, 214–15.

be considered a great good. Thus, escape from evil by necessity involves true freedom to own one's life by making choices that enhance life's meaning.

De-meaning circumstances can become so constricting that one must participate in evil even when one is trying to mitigate evil. One of my undergraduate professors, an expert on the Sudan, told the story of a woman and her three children who had to flee their home but who made it to a refugee camp. After some time, the children, recovering from starvation, began to play like children do. The mother, however, became inconsolable. The relief workers tried to tell her that her children would be fine, that they would live. She finally told them, "You see, I have six children, but I could only carry three." A mother should not have to choose which of her children will live and which will die; she should not have to walk away from her children knowing they will die—these actions undermine the meaning of motherhood; it is a great evil.[33] The same choice that mitigates evil is nonetheless a participation in evil.

Of course not all of our participation in evil is so constricted. One key insight of Judaism and Christianity is that *we are part of the problem*. Evil is not simply something external that happens to us; it is inside us as well. Sometimes I do what I want to do, knowing that it is harmful. In reflecting on an incident where he and some friends stole some pears, the theologian Augustine concluded, "I had no motive for my wickedness except wickedness itself."[34] Even St. Paul found that "when I want to do what is good, evil lies close at hand" (Rom 7:21). Recognizing our own complicity and compromise with evil by repenting of it is necessary for us to experience the good news of the reign of God.[35]

People who experience evil often feel guilt or shame. Guilt is, in part, the feeling of revulsion against our own participation in evil. Feeling guilty is feeling unclean. We want to be clean again, but

33. A fictional account of a similar choice is found in Styron's *Sophie's Choice*.

34. Augustine, *Confessions* 2.9

35. Mark 1:15.

we may not believe that becoming clean is possible. It is important that people not carry more blame than they deserve—and, as we have seen with the Sudanese mother—de-meaning circumstances can severely constrain people and prevent them from doing right. But it is also important not to dismiss guilt as an illusion. People complicit in evil—such as the Sudanese mother—carry the burden of guilt and full healing requires forgiveness, not simply being told that they are not to blame. In our legal society, we blame in order to condemn, but in Christianity, we blame in order to forgive and be reconciled.

Shame, however, is more than guilt; rather, it is *felt* de-meaning. In this sense, it includes guilt, because in guilt we recognize our own actions have de-meaned us as well as others. We simply are not *meant* to de-mean. But shame may be felt when guilt is not present. Shame is typically associated with being de-meaned by others, social disapproval or loss of control over one's life, especially one's body. When someone de-means us whether publicly or privately, we feel shame. Being publicly dressed down or secretly abused will both produce shame, even when we are innocent of wrongdoing. Even life-enhancing choices may incur shame when the society in which we are a part punishes us for good choices. Losing control over one's body is also a common source of shame—consider how something as innocuous as untimely flatulence can cause deep embarrassment. More pointed is the loss of health due to cancer or paralysis that requires one to become completely dependent upon others for even the most basic and intimate tasks. Because our bodies *are* integral to who we are, and not merely a tool of the mind, our loss of control over our bodies de-means us by making us less than who we are meant to be. Of course, sometimes being de-meaned by others, social disapproval, and loss of control are all combined—victims of torture being the clearest example of this sort of evil.

Experiences of people in the sex trade exemplify all of these experiences of evil. Certainly the sex trade is a trap for many. Many girls become prostitutes after being raped—an experience that can encourage a girl to think that all she is good for is to be used by men. Moreover, the ever-present threat of violence by handlers or pimps makes it very difficult to escape.[36] While many women and children are forced or tricked into the trade, some women "choose" it as the best option for making a living given what seems available. Consider a Dominican woman who was married as a young teen and bore her husband several children. But after several years, the husband abandoned her and her children. Without an education or any skills, she went to look for work in the capitol, but could not find any. So she turned to prostitution. This was entirely "voluntary," in the sense that no one else was making her prostitute herself and she is "free" to leave the trade at any time, but her other options are not very good and, in fact, finding a way out soon becomes something very difficult to imagine.

Prostitutes experience both guilt and shame, which make the evil of the sex trade both active and personal. Prostitution meets with widespread social disapproval. Philip Yancey opens his book *What's So Amazing about Grace?* with the story of a prostitute who would never dream of going to a church for help because she is certain they would make her feel worse about herself.[37] Most prostitutes in the Dominican Republic seem reluctant to go to church in the towns where they prostitute themselves (though I have known some to go when invited). But prostitutes are not simply de-meaned by society; prostitution is de-meaning at its very core. I realized this very clearly when visiting a friend in Mexico who runs refuge houses for girls coming out of prostitution. He wanted to show me what some of the secure brothels are like. We went in and three women came out and posed for us to see if we wanted to buy them. It was at that moment that I experienced how demeaning prostitution was, for I was expected to look upon those women as objects, as if I could buy them. The basic premise of prostitution requires the customer to treat the prostitute as if she (or he) is a commodity, something less than human.

36. See, for example, Glenny, *McMafia*, 17–18, 105–7; Jewell, *Escaping the Devil's Bedroom*, 41–45, 58–60; McGill, *Human Traffic*, 76–97; Brock and Thistlethwaite, *Casting Stones*, 160–77.

37. Yancey, *What's So Amazing about Grace?*, 11.

Moreover, women in the sex trade do not have complete control over their own bodies. Many of the women who enter prostitution have already been sexually abused as children; in fact these children are targets for pimps.[38] The alienation from one's own body that this causes certainly makes it easier to contemplate becoming a prostitute. My friend Leslie, who was raped by her father, wrote this about her experience: "The first way that it damaged me was that I saw my body as my worst enemy; my body truly became a prison of horror for me."[39]

The alienation from one's own body permits one to see one's body as something other than oneself, but as a tool to be used and abused. Prostitutes are at significant risk for rape, and, in fact, many men believe they can do what they want with a prostitute because they have paid for it. The Catholic sisters of Las Adoratrices Esclavas del Santísimo Sacramento y de la Caridad in Santiago, Dominican Republic, go to the local hospital every week asking about those prostitutes who have been admitted after having suffered physical abuse at the hands of their customers. They do this because it is so common to find abused prostitutes there. As law professor Catharine MacKinnon said in a debate, "In prostitution, women have sex with men they would never otherwise have sex with. The money thus acts as a form of force, not as a measure of consent."[40] Women in prostitution do not have complete control over their bodies.

Together, the revulsion of prostitution by the public, its inherently de-meaning nature, and the loss of control over one's own body, mean that women in prostitution are often burdened with shame. They feel that they are de-meaned, and this feeling is reinforced throughout the various dimensions of their lives. And because the nature of the sex trade entraps prostitutes, changing

38. Parker, "How Prostitution Works," 11; Raymond et al., *A Comparative Study*, 100–101.

39. Leslie Harley, email to author, 8 June 2009. All translations from this source are by the author.

40. Intelligence Squared, "It's Wrong to Pay for Sex," 28.

their circumstances can be extremely difficult. In these ways, prostitution exemplifies the de-meaning character of evil.

In this chapter, I have set out my thesis that evil is fundamentally a problem of de-meaning and that only a personal, eternal God can save the world from nihilism by giving us a ground for meaning and inviting us to participate in the divine story. Evil is experienced from both human and non-human agents and is felt to be active, personal, and as a constriction of freedom. Our participation in evil, whether as a victim or perpetrator, also brings feelings of guilt and shame. In the next chapter, I will turn to some problems this characterization of evil poses for the Christian defense of God given the existence of de-meaning evil in the world.

# 2

# Evil and Theodicy

In the first chapter, I sketched the character of evil using the sex trade as my primary example. In this chapter I want to reflect briefly on the challenge that de-meaning evil poses for people of faith. The Christian salvation narrative in Scripture teaches us that God is at work in the world to defeat evil. When evil seems victorious, faith in God is rightly tested. One response is theodicy—the effort to defend God's existence and goodness in the face of prevailing evil. In this chapter, I want to suggest that a successful defense of God is sometimes impossible because, by its very nature, de-meaning evil constrains God, so that God must sometimes act unjustly toward us. The death and resurrection of Jesus Christ give us hope, however, that God's promises will yet be fulfilled in us even in face of overwhelming horrendous evil. In the end, it is God who must defend God or we will not be able to sustain our faith.

The book of Job paints a portrait of evil's de-meaning quality. By accusing Job with a lie, Satan de-meaned him. In the heavenly court, God praised Job, declaring him a "blameless and upright man who fears God and turns away from evil" and noting that "there is no one like him on the earth" (Job 1:8). But Satan cast doubt on God's claim, inciting God to destroy Job "for no reason" (Job 2:3). Soon, Job himself sits on the brink of the abyss, feeling his life de-meaned. He believes it would have been better to have never been born than to be abandoned by God as he had been (Job 3). Moreover, Job used images like that of the "Pit" to indicate how thoroughly his life had become a living death.[1] We sense in these exchanges both the "nothingness" of evil and its personal force.

It is important to note that the *reason* God destroyed Job is made clear right from the start: to demonstrate and glorify Job's goodness. The author of the book considered this a good purpose, for it cut to the heart of the meaning of Job's life. Job ought to be praised precisely because his life is well lived and meant something to God and others. In fact, it seems that God drew Satan's attention to Job as an apologia for goodness—a demonstration of its possibility. Satan would have none of it; all good is doubted. But if Job could be vindicated, Satan's justification for his own rebellion would have been undermined—in fact, it will have been shown to be the sham that it is. Moreover, the vindication of Job will bring Job glory in the heavenly court as well as validate God's own word. These are high stakes. Moreover, the nature of the situation precluded Job from knowing the reason evil befalls him. It is not just that Job did not know the reason for his suffering; he *could not* know it or the entire test would fail to achieve the good of Job's and God's vindication.

Suffering, as portrayed in the book of Job, is something God directs. God claimed that he destroyed Job, even though it was at the instigation of Satan (Job 2:3). At no point in Job's accusations against God did God plead innocent as the source of Job's destruction; rather, God assumed all of the responsibility. This responsibility for suffering is not, however, assumed in such a way as to challenge the fundamental goodness of God for the author of the book. Rather, God defeats evil by incorporating suffering into a larger narrative of ultimate goodness for those whose faith is in him. Suffering is not ultimately de-meaning.

One of the insights I wish to suggest from understanding evil as de-meaning is that evil in and of itself is and must be inexplicable. One cannot "make sense" of evil; it is by its very nature

1. Cf. Job 9:31, 17:14; Levenson, *Resurrection and the Restoration of Israel*, 68–71.

meaningless. But meaning can always be made of peoples' lives. That is, meaning is always rooted in *something*—that is, in good. So, on one hand, we must say that evil is insensible; while on the other hand, healing (or re-meaning) is always possible for a *person*, even in the face of the most horrendous evils.

Because healing is possible does not mean it is guaranteed. Lurking in the background of the Job story is the Satan figure who refused to submit to goodness by responding cynically rather than faithfully. It is certainly possible—and indeed the rest of Scripture suggests it is quite likely—that, tragically, some evil will remain unredeemed, though the book of Job and the Scripture as a whole teach that those who respond to God in faith have nothing to fear from evil.

Yet another feature of Job relevant for our discussion is the contrast between Job's response and that of his three friends. Job accused God of unjustly becoming his enemy, leaving him alone and overpowered; his three friends defended the mercy and justice of God. In effect, the friends offer Job a theodicy—a defense of the justice of God. This theodicy was quite orthodox: God is trustworthy; he does great things; he raises the lowly and saves the needy. Accepting God's discipline heals us, and God will save Job, too, if Job submits. Eliphaz and his friends have experienced God's grace and know its truth (Job 5). In all of the long centuries since the book of Job was written, one can hardly find a better theodicy than that offered by Eliphaz. Yet God's wrath was kindled against Eliphaz and his friends for not speaking rightly about God (Job 42:7)!

Let those who seek to justify God beware. In the heavenly court God declared his *injustice* toward Job by saying that he had destroyed Job without reason. God was not justified in his actions against Job, and so Job's accusations against God are right speech. Job was in the right, and God in the wrong. What sense are we to make of this?

I want to hold this question in mind while turning briefly to consider the limits of theodicy in light of the Holocaust—or any other horrendous evil. Rabbi and theologian Irving Greenberg, reflecting on how the Germans would sometimes throw children alive into the furnaces, set forth the following criterion for speech: "No statement, theological or otherwise, should be made that would not be credible in the presence of burning children."[2]

Now this is an impossible criterion against which to measure the intelligibility of speech including theological speech. Our praise of God and gratitude toward God should not be held hostage to evil. To do so would give evil a sort of perverse victory by de-meaning all speech. On the other hand, and this is important, the reality of burning children demonstrates the seriousness the problem of evil has for the believer. Years later, Greenberg revisited his criterion, and I believe his deeper reflection illuminates the challenges evil presents for the faithful. He wrote: "In the presence of burning children, how could one talk of a loving God? I once wrote that no theological statement should be made that would not be credible in the presence of burning children. What could you say about God when a child is burning alive? My answer is there's nothing to say. If there's anything you can do, jump into that pit and pull the child out. And if you can heal that child, if you can pour oil on their burns, then you are making a statement about God."[3]

In the presence of evil, what is important is not speech, but action. We do what we can to mitigate evil. But our faith is still weakened because we have not seen God act to mitigate evil. How do we follow that God? Greenberg continues:

> The answer is you live torn. At one point, the way I put it was that my faith is shattered, but then I was reminded of a famous line of Rabbi Nachman's, the great Hasidic rebbe of Breslov, who once said, "No heart is so whole as a broken heart." So, I came to believe that maybe "no faith is so whole as a broken faith," and I could, in a sense, admire people who responded to the Holocaust by losing their faith, because their passion, their love of God and of people made it impossible to say empty words about God. I felt more sympathy for them than I did for people

2. Greenberg, "Cloud of Smoke," 23.
3. Greenberg, "Easing the Divine Suffering," 67.

> who went on praying as if nothing had ever changed, as if one could talk complacently and confidently about a God who exists self-evidently, as if that's true. It just couldn't be.[4]

Whatever we say must be said with humility and grace. If the book of Job was written for the sort of horrendous evil found in the Holocaust—or the sex trade—then we are reminded how easy it is to talk about God "complacently and confidently," just as Job's friends did.

What the book of Job does not do is explain evil. I have argued that evil itself is fundamentally meaningless and remains on that level inexplicable. But one thing the book of Job does suggest is that, for God, there is distinction between evil as de-meaning and evil as injustice. In order to prevent Job's de-meaning at the hands of his accuser, God acts unjustly toward Job. Job's friends are determined to defend God's justice by proffering a theodicy, but God seems to desire that they defend Job *against* God by speaking truly about God's injustice. For in Job's case, it is only through the injustice of God that the evil of de-meaning is overcome and defeated.

If I am correct in my interpretation of Job, then a theodicy of God's *justice* in the face of horrendous evil is, quite frankly, the wrong approach. Instead we ought to label the Holocaust for what it is: God's injustice toward the Jews. Such a declaration, however, is not meant to abandon all hope for resurrection, reconciliation, and healing for the children burned alive or any of the other horrendous acts of evil—but it does align us with those who have suffered because God did not come to their rescue, and, according to Job, this seems to be where God wants us to be.

The book of Job does have something very important to teach us about our response to God when faced with his injustice. The response that God longs for is the response of faith. What Job needed was not an explanation of the evil that befell him; he needed to know that the God of faith had not abandoned him. Some scholars have suggested that Job did not receive the answer

4. Ibid., 68.

he was looking for and was rather cowed by God's declarations of his power. This seems to me to be a false reading for it does not explain Job's submission. Eleonore Stump has argued that

> it is a mistake . . . to characterize God's speeches as demonstrating nothing but God's power over creation. The speeches certainly do show God's power; but, equally importantly, they show God having personal interactions with all of his creatures. He relates to everything he has made on a face-to-face basis, as it were; and in these personal interactions, God deals maternally with his creatures, from the sea and rain to the raven and the donkey and even the monstrous behemoth and leviathan. He brings them out of the womb, swaddles, feeds, and guides them, and even plays with them. Most importantly, he talks to them; and somehow, in some sense or other, they talk to him in return. These speeches thus show God as more than powerful; they show him as personally and intimately involved with his creation; they portray him as having a mother's care towards all his creatures, even the inanimate ones.[5]

Seeing God face-to-face and hearing assurances of his deep care for one personally *does* seem sufficient to explain Job's humility. One senses that Job longed to submit, but God's rejection of him had made that impossible. When God revealed himself to Job, then Job *knew* that he, too, was still under God's personal care and not cast off. His heart's desire—and the meaning of his life—were still secure.

The "answer" to the problem of evil is, then, not in understanding, but in faith. Stump went on to argue, rightly I believe, that this answer is not a faith in facts about God or the sort of belief that concurs "that God exists, that he is powerful, that he can arrange our lives as he likes, that he does not arrange them as we like, and that we have to accept it at his hand, with whatever patience we can muster, because he is God." Rather faith is "believing that God is really good and so keeps his promises."[6] Make no mistake:

5. Stump, "Faith and the Problem of Evil," 522.

6. Ibid., 549.

this sort of faith is not easy, nor does it lessen the pain. We can sympathize as Rabbi Greenberg does with those who lose faith in face of horrendous evil. May we not be similarly tested!

We might still ask, how can injustice promote healing? Does not injustice also de-mean? Certainly it is often so. This is because injustice contradicts a person's rights. Here we are especially concerned with those rights that exist because God loves us. Thus, we all have an inherent right to respect due us because we are God's special creation, deeply loved by God. For us, rights are useful shorthand for understanding right relation with each other and with God. I cannot be in right relationship with God unless I choose to love God freely. Thus, religious liberty—the right to practice one's religion without interference—is a prerequisite for right relationship with God, even if many people do not enjoy such a relationship. What the right to religious liberty does is help us think about our obligations and claims toward each other. Because God must be loved and worshipped freely, I must not coerce another to believe or worship in a way contrary to their will. Rights are useful in helping us adjudicate certain conflicting claims against each other.

In our relationship with God, however, our rights do not serve quite the same function. Nonetheless, because God loves us and has made promises toward us, we do have certain rights and may make certain claims against God. In fact, God's promises are sufficiently great that we might claim that God has an obligation to resurrect us so that his promises might be fulfilled in our lives. Indeed it is difficult to imagine how God's promises could be fulfilled without such a resurrection. But in saying this, we have now acknowledged that, *in this life*, God's promises toward us are not fully fulfilled. What claims can we assert against God here and now?

Job certainly asserted the claim that God must not destroy him as if he was an enemy of God. This claim was implicitly asserted on the obligations created by God's friendship and mercy. Because God praised Job for right speech, it seems that God legitimized this claim. Yet, God could not (for a time) actualize this claim without Job and God being de-meaned. It seems, then, that the very nature of evil sometimes constrains God's ability to act justly until such time as evil is defeated. Yet, even the defeat of evil must be done with mercy for those trapped in it, and thus (if I may turn around Theodore Parker's phrase), though the arc of the moral universe bends toward justice, it is very long.[7]

Rights and justice are both concerned with right relationship between and among humans, but also between people and God. As I have argued, the meaning of our lives cannot be disentangled from relationship. Right relationship is always grounded in love. And it is here where we must seek an answer to how injustice can defeat de-meaning.

The New Testament teaches us that Jesus Christ's sacrifice on the cross was an act of faith and love. It was also unjust. Jesus asked the Father for the cup to be removed—this suggests that, for Jesus, his death was, in some way, in the hands of the Father, not the Romans (Luke 22:42). I do not think we go wrong in saying that the Father was unjust to the Son in this. The Christ is a Job-figure or, better yet, the experience of Job prefigures that of the Christ. Like Job, Jesus is vindicated and glorified after passing *through* the test. And through his passion, he atoned for the sins of the world and made a new world possible.

In considering the cross, we might say the possibility of right relationship with God is dependent upon injustice. But, if we examine it closely, we see that it is a special kind of injustice—the kind of injustice that heals, rather than destroys. First, we must remember that, according to the Scriptures, Jesus Christ is not an innocent *third* party, but God in the flesh. So while we may say that the Father was unjust to the Son, we cannot say the God was unjust to Jesus because Jesus is also God. As Miroslav Volf has argued, Jesus Christ "stands firmly on the side of the forgiving God, not between the forgiving God and forgiven humanity," and in this way, "The One who was offended bears the burden of the

7. Parker, "Of Justice and the Conscience," 85.

offense."[8] The injustice of the cross makes possible forgiveness, reconciliation, and justice.

Second, the resurrection of Jesus transforms the de-meaning power of evil and death. In so doing, it makes a deeper justice possible. It is only with the resurrection that we can make sense of our lives in face of horrendous evil. By absorbing the de-meaning blow of the cross on our behalf, Jesus Christ makes possible the re-meaning healing power of the resurrection for all. In a real way, then, we participate in the sufferings of Christ and he participates in ours whenever we endure (or are destroyed by) horrendous evil. Yet, even here, our very destruction may reveal our own meaning, defeating the de-meaning power of evil through the grace and love of God. Those who doubt the reality of the resurrection will not be satisfied, of course, for only if we are resurrected may our faith be rewarded and God's promises kept. Christianity without the resurrection is also defeated by evil. Without the resurrection, we have no hope that the evils of the Holocaust, the sex trade, or anything else may be redeemed and healed or God's promises kept.

I must point out something that should be obvious but may not be: if God sometimes acts unjustly toward those he loves, this does not mean that we may. When we act unjustly toward others we are not participating with God, but with Satan in the de-meaning of others and ourselves. Our call is always and everywhere to seek justice, to be merciful, and to help the oppressed. Nor does God the Father model child abuse in his refusal to rescue Jesus from the cross. In the coming kingdom of God the death and resurrection of Jesus advances, there will be no child abuse. We must not be complicit in it now, either by abusing children ourselves or encouraging others to remain in abusive situations as examples of patience and humility. To justify our own injustice by appealing to the injustice of God is to misunderstand the Trinity and the mystery of God's grace and justice. For even in God's injustice toward us, God works mysteriously to defeat evil; whereas our unjust acts oppose God and promote our own destruction and de-meaning.

8. Volf, *Free of Charge*, 145.

On the other hand, the example of Christ and his presence with us does mean that we need not fear death or horrendous evil. That is, out of love, we might take upon ourselves the abuse of the oppressor so that its power can be nullified through our resurrection. We must not mistake self-sacrifice for self-abnegation. Self-sacrifice is a free choice of love and hope. Remaining in an abusive situation is most often not motivated by love, but by fear. The healthy do not seek to be stepped on. Our nonviolent nonresistance is aggressive in its hope and love, not passive in despair. We must not seek martyrdom. But should it come to us, we need not fear it, and may even embrace it in joy, as our own martyrs teach us.

In the end, the difficulty for the theodicist is that God must answer for God. Too often we act as if we can conjure God's appearance for others, but when God does not appear as we desire, our fear gets the better of us and we begin to make excuses for God. Truly, unless one experiences God in Jesus Christ, Christianity will not make sense. We can invite people into our communities of love, but we cannot manufacture the experience of God for them. We simply must wait on God and have faith that he will keep his promises.

To someone who does not believe, the refrain to "just have faith," however nuanced, is unlikely to be satisfactory (unless, perhaps, accompanied by an experience of God—an experience the apologist cannot manufacture). But de-meaning evil poses even greater problems for an atheistic worldview, problems we will examine in the next chapter.

# 3

# Evil, Atheism, and the Problem of Healing

FOR SOME, THE "PROBLEM of evil" is the atheist trump card against Christianity. Given the quality and quantity of evil in the world, belief in God is simply impossible, they say. In this chapter, I wish to respond briefly to these challenges and show how weak they are. In fact, it is Christianity, not atheism, that offers both a realistic vision of evil and the hope that it may be overcome. In order to disbelieve in God, atheists must either deny evil or hope, as well as credible testimonies of healing in face of horrendous evil. This "problem of healing" poses a serious intellectual challenge to morally sensitive atheists.

Let us consider J. L. Mackie's logic puzzle: "God is omnipotent; God is wholly good; and yet evil exists. There seems to be some contradiction between these three propositions."[1] Alvin Plantinga has argued that Mackie fails to show the inherent contradiction and thus belief in God may remain rational.[2] Plantinga's logic is engaging, but I will argue that, by introducing a premise about hope, we reveal a more serious contradiction the atheist must face.

1. Mackie, "Evil and Omnipotence," 89.
2. Plantinga, "The Free Will Defense."

Let's accept the atheist's premise: (1) a loving, all-powerful God does *not* exist. Let's also accept the atheist's premise that evil exists. I realize that the atheist need not accept this premise—in fact many do not. I want to return to this idea below, but in order to make the contradiction clear, we need to propose it. However, I want to rephrase the premise. Rather than saying merely that "evil exists," I want to propose a substitute: (2) evil threatens both my existence and the meaning of my life. If evil exists, and if it is gratuitous, as Rowe believes, then by its very nature it must threaten our existence and meaning. If we only state that evil exists, we might lose sight of what is at stake. Now, the third premise I wish to add is this: (3) I have hope that evil may be overcome and my life will have meaning. Placing them side by side, we have:

(1) No loving, all-powerful God exists.

(2) Evil threatens both my existence and the meaning of my life.

(3) I have hope that evil may be overcome and my life will have meaning.

I suggest that all three cannot be true and that the atheist, to remain an atheist, must deny either (2) or (3). Hope is never ungrounded—in order to have hope, one must have the objective possibility that what one hopes may become true. What I will argue is that atheism has no grounds for hope sufficient to overcome the threat of horrendous evil.

First, however, I want to revise Mackie's argument to show that for the Christian, a contradiction no longer exists. Here it is:

(1a*) God is omnipotent.

(1b*) God is good.

(2) Evil threatens both my existence and the meaning of my life.

(3) I have hope that evil may be overcome and my life will have meaning.

I believe that I am not being unfair to Mackie to suggest that this is essentially his argument with the addition of premise (3). But when phrased this way, the argument takes on a whole new dimension. While this argument does not necessarily mitigate any existential suffering, it is logically consistent. For, if Christianity is true and God is good, loving, and all-powerful, then we certainly ought to hope that evil will be defeated and our lives will have meaning.

I think this brings us closer to seeing why so few Christians actually deny Mackie's premise that evil exists. Certainly, on logical grounds, this would be the easiest way out while still preserving a good, omnipotent God. So why are Christians so loathe to eliminate it? The entire Christian narrative is predicated on the fact that a loving, all-powerful God is at work in the world to defeat evil. If a Christian gives up the premise that evil exists and poses a real existential threat to us, then we must give up Christianity. This premise is as integral to Christianity as the other premises about the character of God. Place all three premises together and we come to the heart of the Christian story: there is hope in face of great evil.

Turning back to my argument, I seek to demonstrate a contradiction between disbelieving in God while believing in both evil and hope. One popular way out of this apparent contradiction is simply to deny that evil exists. The denial of evil is a necessary consequence of the denial of moral objectivity, an approach taken by Friedrich Nietzsche and J. L. Mackie. Nietzsche declared, "There are altogether no moral facts,"[3] and Mackie argued forcefully that "there are no objective values."[4] These premises are necessary in order to defend the idea that we should create our own ethics. For Nietzsche this meant rejecting the Christian "slave" morality, whereas Mackie actually wished to keep most of this morality.[5]

3. Nietzsche, "The 'Improvers' of Mankind," 501.

4. Mackie, *Ethics*, 15.

5. For example, Mackie thought truth-telling and promise-keeping to be necessary for the general happiness, although at times these might conflict with self-interest. In some respects, Mackie does undermine Christian morality, especially the idea that all humans are of infinite worth. See Mackie, *Ethics*, 169–72. Nietzsche wrote in response to George Eliot: "When the English actually believe that they know 'intuitively' what is good and evil, when they therefore suppose that they no longer require Christianity as the guarantee of morality, we merely witness the *effects* of the dominion of the Christian value

But criticizing either of their philosophies of ethics is beyond the scope of this essay. Instead, I want to focus on what the denial of moral objectivity does for the idea of evil.

I hold that the denial of any sort of transcendent moral order affirms the *objective* victory of evil. Here is why: the atheist certainly does not deny the existence of meaning. As I have argued in chapter 1, humans are meaning-makers whether or not God exists, and the atheist certainly recognizes this. The problem for the atheist is not that there is no meaning now; the problem is that the abyss will be victorious. Consider what the best science teaches us about naturalistic eschatology: the universe will become uninhabitable; all life will die. That is to say, one day there will be no more meaning-makers alive.

With the death of all meaning-makers comes the death of all meaning. That is, the history of humanity and of every individual life will no longer hold any meaning. Everything that once held meaning will be de-meaned. Since I have argued that de-meaning is a central characteristic of evil, then what atheistic eschatology guarantees us is the absolute assurance of the objective victory of evil over all.

Of course the atheist is free to deny that this is evil—that is, the atheist may deny that *anything* is evil. It is simply our personal preference or desire that meaning continue. We must redefine evil to mean that which we do not personally prefer. I believe this proposal has three serious flaws.

First, it impoverishes language. When people say that something is "evil," or "wrong," they mean something more than "I (or we) do not prefer this." We are, in fact, appealing to a transcendent moral order. Mackie knew that he was going against the grain and has proposed creative explanations for how this transcendent

---

judgment and an expression of the strength and depth of the dominion: such that the origin of the English morality has been forgotten, such that the very conditional character of its right to existence is no longer felt" ("Skirmishes of an Untimely Man," 516). Nietzsche called Christian morality "the most malignant form of the will to lie, the real Circe of humanity—that which *corrupted* humanity" ("Why I Am a Destiny," 788).

appeal might have developed naturally in human societies.[6] In the end, he must claim that a whole realm of everyday language does not mean what we think it means. This is not fatal to his project, but it is not very satisfactory.

Second, and more threatening for Mackie's denial of a transcendent moral order, is the nearly universal human agreement about the reality and character of evil. By appealing to the plurality of visions for the good life, Mackie argued that the "good" could not be objectively defined. But he did recognize that there was substantial agreement about "evils"—those things that threaten all competing visions of the good life. I have argued in chapter 1 that de-meaning is *the* universal and objective threat to all goods. But Mackie cannot have it both ways; he cannot hold that good is subjective while evil is objective; he must either deny evil (as I believe he does) or his rejection of transcendent values may be called into question. The problem with denying evil is that one must deny that death is a problem for meaning—that is, for all subjective understandings of good. Because death is an objective fact, I think his denial of evil results in a refusal to take evil very seriously.

Finally, the future vision of the death of everything coupled with the inability to take evil seriously has dangerous ethical consequences. What is needed to stand against the evils of the world is courage, and courage depends on hope that evil may be overcome. Yet, if atheistic naturalism is right in believing that all value and meaning will cease and good and evil are projections of our personal preferences, then what grounds courage? Why risk one's life to help children out of prostitution or free the slaves? In the end, death will swallow everything. Thus, while the denial of evil is not logically impossible, it seems to me to amount to a denial of our humanity and a capitulation to death.

It is more tempting, if not more promising, for the atheist to argue that other sources of hope are surer than that offered by Christianity. Bertrand Russell, who I have had occasion to mention earlier, is one atheist who took this course. Russell was an indefatigable campaigner against evils of his day, especially war

6. Mackie, *Ethics*, 83–102.

and the threat of nuclear holocaust. He did not deny evil; he took it seriously enough to oppose it and called upon others to oppose it too.

For Russell, ethics are utilitarian, but not in the sense of "enlightened self-interest" as Jeremy Bentham would have it, but in the Aristotelian sense that they are means to achieve goals. Ethics are always "tested by examining whether they tend to realize ends that we desire."[7] Russell uses *desire* and rejects *oughtness*; for what one "'ought' to desire is merely what someone else wishes us to desire." Rightness or wrongness has its source in the social order. Yet the social order is not absolute either. The good life "is inspired by love and guided by knowledge."[8] Therefore morality "must be examined with a view to seeing whether it is such as wisdom and benevolence would have decreed."[9] Russell leaves room for improving the social order through reform by testing it against wisdom informed by scientific knowledge.

Russell's hope for a better world was clear: rational thinking by the educated elite. He believed that scientists not only should but could "diminish the magnitude of evil" by providing leadership and directing science toward beneficial, rather than harmful, purposes.[10] Thanks to scientific thinking, real moral progress was possible. He proclaimed, "Science can, if it chooses, enable our grandchildren to live the good life, by giving them knowledge, self-control and characters productive of harmony rather than strife. At present it is teaching our children to kill each other, because many men of science are willing to sacrifice the future of mankind to their own momentary prosperity. But this phase will pass when men have acquired the same domination over their own passions that they already have over the physical forces of the external world. Then at last we shall have won our freedom."[11]

7. Russell, "What I Believe," 374.
8. Ibid., 376–77.
9. Ibid., 377.
10. Russell, "The Social Responsibilities of Scientists," 230–31.
11. Russell, "What I Believe," 390.

It is no surprise that other atheists have taken a similar path. Science is demonstrably progressive and has brought humanity—or substantial parts of it—great material blessings. Moreover, science has also been effective at healing people's bodies and promoting longer life expectancy. Two centuries of extraordinary scientific progress has encouraged in us a sense that continued progress is certain and unlimited. Faith in the omnipotence of science is evident in the atheist Islam's claim that even after the dissolution of supermassive black holes a google years from now, "there will always be . . . a constantly expanding domain of life, consciousness and memory."[12]

Yet Russell's hopes are misplaced. First and most importantly, Russell has misunderstood the nature of evil. He certainly believed in its existence, and he took it seriously, but he failed, it seems, to grasp the full scope of its powers. For Russell, evil seems to have been that which threatened the good life, as Russell defined it. This included both external threats, like nuclear war, and also internal flaws, like ignorance. While this is true insofar as it goes, evil is more threatening than that—for, in fact, many people have not lived the good life and this means evil has had the victory in their lives.

Russell was not a relativist despite his claims that ultimately *ought* and *should* were dependent upon a relative social authority. In fact, Russell's works are filled with all sorts of *oughts* and *shoulds* that he posits as if they are universal. He told educators that "[e]ducation ought to foster the wish for truth"[13] and politicians that "the West ought to alleviate abject poverty."[14] He declared that we cannot tell the conscientious objector that "he ought not to act as his conscience dictates."[15] Even morality itself "ought not to be such as to make instinctive happiness impossible."[16] This is not the language of a consistent relativist. Rather, Russell seems to have

12. Islam, *The Ultimate Fate of the Universe*, 111.

13. Russell, "Education," 406.

14. Russell, "Why I Am Not a Communist," 481.

15. Russell, "Individual and Social Ethics," 358.

16. Russell, "What I Believe," 380.

believed that philosophical thinking can get us partway—but only partway—to an objective understanding of reality.[17]

I do not wish to argue the idea that once one has accepted the idea of *oughtness* (or lives as if one accepts it), then one has moved beyond a strictly naturalist and godless universe. Better philosophers than I have already done this, and I find their arguments compelling.[18] What I do wish to show, however, is that Russell assumes quite correctly that people and their actions have purpose and meaning. But when evil is understood as *meaninglessness*, the atheist, like Russell, has little recourse because meaning depends, not only upon purpose and will but also upon an eternal and personal being who continues to hold it. Because, in Russell's universe, no such being exists, neither does hope exist.

Russell was certainly committed to human salvation by turning science and scientific thinking to the promotion of the good life, as he understood it. But what of all of those who perished without having experienced this goodness? How does the possibility that one day all will enjoy a good life redeem the torture of small children? The atheist can either suggest that the evils that befall innocent children are either unredeemable or redeemed through the warning and inspiration they offer us as we work toward creating a utopian future. If the former, then we have no ground for hope that good will prevail over past or most present evil. Tragedy is written in stone. If the latter, then we have merely turned ourselves into the god who builds a perfect world on the sufferings of children, a god that Ivan Karamazov rejects.[19] It is one thing to reject the transcendent and personal God of Christianity as a moral protest against the evil God permits, but if *we* are that very same god—the very god that builds a utopia on the backs of tortured children—then should not our protest result in a *withdrawal* of support from the utopian project? And if we withdraw support, then have we not given evil the victory by default?

17. Russell, *My Philosophical Development*, 158.

18. See, for example, Linville, "The Moral Argument."

19. Dostoyevsky, *The Brothers Karamazov*, 226.

We have seen already that, for Russell, the highest purpose of humanity can only be to "cherish lofty thoughts" and to "sustain the world that [our] ideals have fashioned," though it is, in fact, doomed.[20] This is a purpose in which much of humanity simply cannot take part and, while it may appeal to our sense of courage in good times, seems to me to leave one without the sustaining hope to endure evil times. Either we must forget that children are still burned, raped, and hacked apart with machetes or else we must lose hope. In the end, death will swallow all, and its victory will be eternal.

Russell's hope in science and scientists also seems misplaced. The idea that the rationalistic, scientific elite can really drive the establishment of a world of love and peace seems to me to be unwarranted. I do not wish to deny the possibility that science can make (and has made) a *contribution* to a better world, but it seems to me that scientists as a whole are unlikely to prove to be the world's saviors. Scientists are not immune from those feelings and desires that lead to human conflict; science was necessary to create weapons of mass destruction. Much of modern Western science fiction, beginning with Mary Shelley's *Frankenstein*, warns us that moral hubris can be found among scientists. And while most scientists are concerned about conducting research in life-affirming and socially acceptable ways, moral controversies exist over such issues as nuclear weapons, animal testing, DNA manipulation, stem cells, and human cloning.

Therefore, if the atheist wishes to avoid the contradiction, the best approach may be to deny the third premise: "I have hope that evil may be overcome and my life will have meaning." Albert Camus took this approach in his brilliant work, *The Plague*. Set in Oran during an outbreak of bubonic plague, the central character, Dr. Rieux, struggles to fight against evil as represented by the plague. Camus, through Rieux, makes it clear that evil must be opposed, and he criticized attempts to defend the intelligibility of evil: "What's true of all evils in the world is true of the plague as well. It helps men to rise above themselves. All the same, when you

20. Russell, "A Free Man's Worship," 47.

see the misery it brings, you'd need to be a madman, or a coward, or stone blind to give in tamely to the plague."[21]

While good can come out of evil, one should nonetheless "try to relieve suffering before trying to point out its excellence."[22] For Rieux—and Camus—creation as it is must be fought against. God is rejected because creation is rejected. As Rieux protests, "[S]ince the order of the world is shaped by death, mightn't it be better for God if we refuse to believe in Him and struggle with all our might against death, without raising our eyes toward the heaven where He sits in silence?"[23] The doctor is not ignorant of what this means. Because the power of death is greater than the power of life, Rieux and all those who follow his example must face "a never ending defeat."[24]

What Camus praises is a certain ethical stance against death. He knows that many Christians participate in this struggle, and, in fact, the character of Father Paneloux who originally preached about the plague's meaning ultimately gives his own life working against it. In one important scene Father Paneloux and Dr. Rieux engage in a difficult conversation after having together watched a child die slowly. After some initial sharp words, Rieux, the atheist, affirms, "We're working side by side for something that unites us—beyond blasphemy and prayers. And it's the only thing that matters."[25] It is not grace or faith, but healing that is most important.

One cannot help but admire Camus's portrayal of courage without hope, as well as his ecumenism in his recognition of ethical solidarity between believers and non-believers. Nonetheless, I believe his stance is flawed for two reasons. First, courage without hope is not logical; it is merely a personal preference, and one that most will not be able to sustain. Second, Rieux's defiance is still not meaningful if there is no meaning. In fact, it only makes sense *if* there is a God who takes an active interest in the world.

21. Camus, *The Plague*, 115.

22. Ibid., 116.

23. Ibid., 117–18.

24. Ibid., 118.

25. Ibid., 197.

That is, Rieux's hopeless struggle against evil and his anger at the silent God that does not exist still *depends* upon the existence of that God. To reject belief in God because it is morally outrageous is to love that very same God. Nor is it possible to sustain such admirable ethics without a culture that believes that evil must be opposed and that we had hope in so doing. That is, without Christianity, Camus would not have had the moral imagination required to write *The Plague*.

This does not make Christianity true by default. Atheists are certainly logically consistent if they wish to deny hope. What it does do is show how *attractive* the Christian narrative is. The Christian proclaims that salvation *is* possible, the atheist that we must suffer a neverending defeat. The question then becomes: Is salvation really possible? Does healing in spite of horrendous evil actually happen? Because if salvation is possible then the atheist has a problem: the problem of healing. A worldview that either denies evil or denies hope will not be able to explain it.

Healing in the face of horrendous evil is possible. I turn again to the story of my friend, Leslie.

Broken, Leslie had finally decided to end her life. She had been abused, raped, prostituted, and almost killed. Yet, she wrote, "No one, not even my worst enemy wanted my death more than I wanted it; no one damaged me or caused me more pain than I inflicted on myself, especially against my body."[26] She hated her own body; she despised herself. Her emotions were characterized by fear, anger, guilt, shame, and pain. She used drugs and alcohol to numb the pain, but found that the pain was always there when she returned. She wrote that she carried guilt

> for the sexual abuse in my childhood; for the rape in my adolescence; for the physical abuse and attempted murder against me; for having been rejected by the nuns to enter the convent; for having been an atheist and a communist; for my bad decisions in choosing partners; for my promiscuity; for the permanent physical damage I carry in my body from being abused and raped; for

26. Leslie Harley, email to author, 8 June 2009.

> having wasted my talent for throwing overboard a career and a steady job; for having wasted time on unproductive and self-destructive activities; for being unable to manage money and property when I was addicted to drugs; for having aborted my first child; for hurting so many people; for conceiving my children without true love; for having used drugs, snuff and alcohol during my pregnancies; for having worked in prostitution for so many years; for stealing; for having used drugs to destroy my body; for having hurt my body in the sex trade; for lying to my family over the years while working as a prostitute and for leaving my children during those years; for my attempts at suicide; for failing to build healthy, lasting friendships; and for preferring to be alone than to risk being hurt.[27]

And of the pain, even years later, she said: "Pain is a feeling that leaves me bedridden and empty-handed. It was terrible to face my memories: I lost my childhood; I lost my innocence; I lost my parents; I lost my adolescence; I lost my dreams; I lost my youth; all lost, lost, lost . . . How can I describe the pain? It is fear, powerlessness, and anger. It is shame, indifference, and despair. It is the abyss. It is the thin boundary between continuing the fight to stay alive or surrendering to seek relief in death."[28]

And so she resolved to kill herself. She was all alone. The appointed day came, and she called a taxi to take her to the place where she had chosen to die.

And then she remembered her sister who had converted to Christ. She called her and asked for help. Her sister took her to meet her pastor and Leslie let herself be rescued. Of Jesus Christ, she said: "He was my savior, the knight of my dreams, that love [I had secretly longed for] in my sleepless nights and despair, Christ was my salvation."[29]

Her journey of healing had only begun, and even today the pain threatens to overwhelm her. She characterizes her journey as

27. Ibid.

28. Ibid.

29. Leslie Harley, email to author, 5 August 2010.

one being guided by God. The lies that her "body is crap" and that it "has no value" are broken by the truths that God made her body good and that he wants to dwell in her body. Guilt for false sins is countered with the truth that she is only responsible for her own sins—and for these she knows that God has forgiven her. The fear that her trauma will still destroy her is met with the truth that, in Christ, nothing evil has the last word, and that he, too, knows pain, even the pain of having his Father abandon him in his hour of deepest need.[30]

She consistently credits the epiphanies and healing moments to the work of God. Of course her healing is nurtured by a supportive community. Yet, she feared depending on others. She described how her willingness to dare to trust others for help came from an experience with God: "Crying in the arms of the Lord I said: 'No one will understand me, nobody cares, nobody is going to love me after coming to know me; please do not make me ask for help, your help is enough for me.' God kept hugging me and saying something like this to my heart: 'The spiritual life is a reflection of your worldly life; the road must be traveled in both directions, from your relationships with others into your relationship with me and from the privacy of our communion to a change with others. You cannot have one without the other.'"[31]

Her testimony is a story of great healing in the face or horrendous evil, of a life nearly destroyed, but saved from the brink of the void. The credit she gives for this healing is first and foremost to the power of God in Jesus Christ. She *has* hope in spite of evil, which did pose a threat to the meaning of her life and her very existence.

How can the atheist explain this? *There are no moral facts?* Certainly such an assertion is absurd. Rather, if one is raped, abused, prostituted, nearly killed, and brought to the very brink of suicide, how is denying good and evil any encouragement? Certainly such a statement *would make the world worse*, not better. There is no hope for healing there.

30. Leslie Harley, email to author, 8 June 2009.

31. Ibid.

*Worship at the shrine that one's own hands have built?* For a victim of abuse, terror, and fear, what shrine is that? How could this be interpreted as anything except the worship of death? For when we suffer horrendous evil at the hands of others, what other shrine can be imagined? Will scientific and rational thinking help give the victim the power to experience healing? Yet certainly we would have had to dismiss as superstition the most incisive and clear-sighted truths that Leslie experienced in communion with God. Even if we accepted that, by some chance, Christians had stumbled upon good, sound psychological advice, this "advice" is *entirely dependent upon the existence of a personal, loving, and forgiving God*. Moreover, the atheist would have to tell the victim that, in order to be fully mature, she must reject the very thing that wrought her healing. This deep ingratitude seems therapeutically unwise, to say the least.

*We are sure to face a neverending defeat?* Is it really possible for most of us to sustain courage against the darkness without hope? Rieux was part of a community that might stand together against the plague, a community deeply influenced by Christian ideas of right and wrong. But Leslie was all alone. Whereas we might be able to stand together—for a while—if we have each other, all alone it seems impossible to me. The godlessness of the society Leslie inhabited before her conversion did not offer any hope for healing—only another round of abuse and sorrow.

We could argue that what began Leslie's healing was not God, but the help of humans, and that her journey was abetted by good psychology, whatever its source. These things are certainly true, but as an explanation they are unconvincing. For Leslie does not believe that any individual person or any community could have saved her. In fact, she had waited for someone to come along and save her during her years of misery. According to her, it was Jesus Christ who rescued her, and it is to him that her gratitude is due. To deny the centrality of her faith in God for her healing is no longer to take her seriously as a witness.

Another option is to take Nietzsche's course and de-mean Leslie. Of the "ascetic priest," he said, "He combats only the suffering itself, the discomfiture of the sufferer, *not* its cause, *not* the real sickness."[32] Nietzsche recognized better than most that the Christian yearning was for meaning. He wrote:

> Apart from the ascetic ideal, man, the human *animal*, had no meaning so far. His existence on earth contained no goal; "why man at all?"—was a question without an answer; the *will* for man and earth was lacking; behind every great human destiny there sounded as a refrain a yet greater "in vain!" *This* is precisely what the ascetic ideal means: that something was *lacking*, that man was surrounded by a fearful *void*—he did not know how to justify, to account for, to affirm himself; he *suffered* from the problem of his meaning. He also suffered otherwise, he was in the main a sickly animal: but his problem was *not* suffering itself, but that there was no answer to the crying question, "*why* do I suffer?"[33]

Because this question so haunted us, Nietzsche argued, we gave meaning to our lives through asceticism—turning our attention inward and bringing "fresh suffering with it, deeper, more inward, more poisonous, more life-destructive suffering."[34] Christianity at its heart expresses "this hatred of the human, and even more of the animal, and more still of the material, this horror of the senses, of reason itself, this fear of happiness and beauty, this longing to get away from all appearance, change, becoming, death, wishing, from longing itself—all this means—let us dare to grasp it—*a will to nothingness*, an aversion to life, a rebellion against the most fundamental presuppositions of life; but it is and remains a *will!* . . . And, to repeat in conclusion what I said at the beginning: man would rather will *nothingness* than *not* will."[35]

From a Nietzschean point of view, what Leslie has done by surrendering herself to God is to hate her own body and life and to will her own destruction.

32. Nietzsche, *On the Genealogy of Morals*, 565–66.

33. Ibid., 598.

34. Ibid.

35. Ibid., 598–99.

I hope it is obvious to even the most determined skeptic that this analysis is absurd. By Leslie's own testimony, it was in life *without* God that she willed nothingness and destruction. Her surrender to Jesus Christ has not resulted in her destruction, but significant progress toward her own healing. She has been lifted out of the pit and now has hope. She claims meaning for her life—a meaning that is grounded in God's love for her. Nietzsche's analysis fails the acid test of history: where he sees hatred, Leslie experiences love. Where he sees fear of happiness and beauty, Leslie experiences courage to accept happiness and beauty. Where he sees an aversion to life, Leslie experiences life anew. In the end, Nietzsche died having gone mad, but Leslie lives and is being made well. If some people really are healed from horrendous evil, then atheism is no longer believable.

If we take Leslie seriously, then atheism suffers from a difficult logical problem. She lends credence to the premises that both evil and hope exist and she shows how these are incompatible with disbelief in God. The atheist can offer no compelling counter-narrative to substitute for Leslie's own story while maintaining the premise that God does not exist. If they admit that moral facts exist independently of the natural world, then they have opened the door to the divine; if they refuse to believe in evil, then they have closed their ears to the world's suffering. And if they admit evil, they can offer no ground for hope for anything better, except the optimistic dreams of philosophers whose own sense of right and wrong is deeply indebted to Jesus Christ.

Leslie is not alone. Healing is at the very heart of the Christian story and an appropriate synonym for salvation. Healing is not simply about making the body well again (though it is certainly about that), but about restoring the meaning of one's life. In this sense, of course, Christianity is deeply indebted to Judaism whose Scriptures proclaim a God of healing. Consider how in the Hebrew Scriptures God's healing power is revealed in opening barren wombs. In so doing, the *meaning* and blessedness of life is healed in the sociocultural context of ancient Israel.[36] Israel's Messiah ought

36. Levenson, *Resurrection and the Restoration of Israel*, 108, 142.

to be a healer—and such is the claim made by Christians for Jesus Christ. Healing is not only central to his mission while he lived, but his disciples believed that his healing work continued into the present because he had been resurrected. In fact, his resurrection is the ultimate ground of hope that evil will be defeated and that its defeat has already begun.[37]

Healing, hope, and meaning were and are driving forces for the spread of Christianity. The power in the Christian faith to effect cures and relief from evil spirits is what the historian Ramsey MacMullen suggested likely initiated many into the Christian faith before Constantine.[38] Nor was this unique to early Christianity. In early medieval Europe, the Christian message came with power to deliver people from evil spirits and to ensure good harvests.[39] In modern Nepal, numbers of Christians have grown from twenty-five in 1950 to over 440,000 at the end of the twentieth century. When a Western missionary asked first generation Christians what brought them to faith, "[t]he most frequent response was that they had experienced difficulties with demons and had tried many remedies, even exorcism attempts by Hindu priests, all to no avail." But converts all "emphasized that it was not so much the act of a person casting a demon out of them that had brought them to faith as the message of the gospel which they believed in their desperation."[40] Throughout the global South, the poor "are less than startled at a society ravaged by epidemics and random violence, deprived of adequate food supplies, unable to trust the drinking water, subject to ever more oppressive policing and internal security." It is these same people who also experience the power of the Christian gospel as a force for liberation and hope.[41] Atheists who are used to confronting the stunted Christian faith of wealthy Westerners forget that Christianity has been so successful because it works. People meet God and are healed.

37. See Porterfield, *Healing in the History of Christianity*, esp. chaps. 1 and 2.

38. MacMullen, *Christianizing the Roman Empire*, 40–42.

39. Fletcher, *The Barbarian Conversion*, 243–45.

40. Pocock et al., *The Changing Face of World Missions*, 193.

41. Jenkins, *The New Faces of Christianity*, 96.

Most atheists, I suspect, will remain unconvinced, perhaps because they have not met any who have been healed in light of great evil. It will be easier to assume that Christianity is a therapeutic placebo, even though such assumptions betray their own ignorance of evil and refusal to take people at their word. Nonetheless, the problem of healing remains for the serious and honest atheist who would remain a logically consistent atheist.

# 4

# Evil and Feminist Theology

In earlier chapters, I have defined the fundamental character of evil as de-meaning and considered the threat that it poses for people of faith and unbelief. I have argued that death is so de-meaning that evil can only be defeated with resurrection, as Christians claim. Yet some people of faith within the Christian tradition have rejected the traditional claims of the Christian faith. In this chapter, I intend to offer preliminary criticism of some feminist theologians by considering how their approach to evil fails to ground final hope for women and others caught in the sex trade. Instead, I will argue that the gospel of traditional orthodox Christianity is really "good news" for these women.

While there is no single feminist theology or approach to evil, all feminist theology desires to promote the liberation of women from arbitrary constraints. The test of this liberation—and thus feminist theology—is the concrete, lived experience of women. Women's experiences are necessarily of critical importance to theological reflection.[1]

Many Christian and post-Christian feminist theologians come from evangelical or traditional Christian homes, and a growing number of thoughtful evangelical pastors and theologians

1. Watson, *Feminist Theology*, 2–3.

encounter feminist thought, both in the academy as well as in the pews. One area of great concern to both feminist and evangelical theologians is the problem of evil. Feminists have critiqued traditional orthodox responses to this problem, but evangelical theologians have not (to my knowledge) engaged feminist thinkers on this topic.[2] Not only does feminist thinking deserve thoughtful criticism, but their work may yield insights for the whole church. While it is unlikely that the great differences between feminist and evangelical theologians will be bridged, discussion may yet prove fruitful to both parties. In this chapter, I hope to begin such a scholarly encounter.

There is no one feminist theology of evil, nor are all feminist theologies irreconcilable with my own. For example, Nel Noddings's understanding of evil as pain, separation, and helplessness has much to commend it, even if I find her portrayal of Christianity as repressive foreign to my experience.[3] She assumed that Christianity is a social construct and not an encounter with a transcendent God who really is seeking to redeem and heal people. Consequently, my fundamental issue with her is not how she framed the problem of evil as much as how she resolved it—or failed to do so. Time and space limitations prevent me from considering Noddings or many other creative feminist thinkers, though I believe a comprehensive critical treatment of the feminist theology of evil would be useful.

For this preliminary analysis of evil in feminist theology, I intend to examine two works: *Journeys by Heart: A Christology of Erotic Power* by Rita Nakashima Brock and *Proverbs of Ashes: Violence, Redemptive Suffering and the Search for What Saves Us* by Brock and Rebecca Ann Parker. I recognize that Brock (along with Susan Thistlethwaite) has written specifically and thoughtfully about the sex trade in *Casting Stones: Prostitution and Liberation in Asia and the United States* (1996). Indeed, reading this book was

2. For example, evangelical scholar Peterson's collection of essays on the problem of evil does not include any feminist theologians. See Peterson, *The Problem of Evil.*

3. Noddings, *Women and Evil.*

influential in setting me on a course to try to help victims of the sex trade. Nonetheless, I will be setting it aside for this preliminary investigation to focus more specifically on the problem of evil. In this chapter, I will examine and critique Brock and Parker's understanding of evil, salvation, and ethics as reflected in *Journeys by Heart* and *Proverbs of Ashes*.

We ought to acknowledge that one of the most important differences between feminist and traditional orthodox or evangelical theologians is their approach to Scripture. Some feminists are not able to surrender themselves to Scripture. The primary source for feminist theology is women's experience, not Scripture. When these experiences conflict or seem to conflict with what the Scripture teaches, then the Scripture is understood as an obstacle to the dignity of women. Of course, traditional theologians may feel the same tension between women's experience and the Scriptures, but, because of their commitment to the Scripture as an authority, the conflict must be lived through in a way that denies neither the authority of Scripture nor the dignity of women, a sometimes difficult task. While my criticisms will from time to time touch on how feminist theologians interpret Scripture, I include no thoroughgoing criticism of feminist hermeneutics—a task that has already been taken up by abler scholars.[4] Nonetheless, the different approaches to the Scripture will necessarily result in very different methods and conclusions, though we may yet learn from each other despite this fundamental difference.

My criticisms of my feminist dialogue partners are not primarily over their use of Scripture but rather are grounded in conflicting understandings of evil and how it can be defeated. In short, I contend that the theology of Rita Nakashima Brock and Rebecca Parker does not take evil seriously enough. Consequently, their proposed solution is not able to overcome evil or give much hope for healing.

Brock and Parker diminish evil when they conflate it with "patriarchy." This conflation diminishes evil for several reasons. First, patriarchy is poorly defined and generally viewed through

4. For example, see Kimel, *Speaking the Christian God.*

the eyes of victims of abuse, usually children, and this abuse is often at the hands of men. This viewpoint is helpful for articulating the power and influence of de-meaning systems, but the result is a downplaying of human sin for fear of aggravating evil through concepts of "blame" and "guilt," which they consider patriarchal tools of control. So while Brock and Parker took systems of evil seriously, their view of evil is unbalanced because they minimized our personal responsibility for it.

Brock demonstrated sensitivity to how evil can infect systems and societies. She understood that evil is global in scale and that it seeks to obliterate the meaning of many, if not most, human lives.[5] Though she knows also that "patriarchy is not the only cause of human evil and suffering," she focused her attention on it.[6] She followed Gerda Lerner in defining patriarchy as "male dominance over women" in the family and in society. While women need not be without power or rights, the power differential between men and women means women are always vulnerable to male abuse.[7] Moreover, both Brock and Parker have experienced abuse at the hands of men and worked with women and children who have experienced abuse. Parker was raped repeatedly as a child by a neighbor, and her moving testimony illuminates how the devastation of abuse can influence one's view of what happened between God the Father and the Son, Jesus Christ, on the cross.[8] Brock and Parker offer trenchant criticism of the church's complicity in creating a "patriarchal" world where children are raped.

It is a much-needed perspective, but they failed to fully substantiate their criticism. I wish to tread carefully here because I fear any counter-criticism will be seen as a vehicle for excusing Christians from reflecting on their own sin and silence in the face of child abuse and other evils in our society. Moreover, we who have not experienced abuse *need* to hear their stories, and as Brock and Parker recommend, we need to create communities of

5. Brock, *Journeys by Heart*, 1.

6. Ibid., 3.

7. Ibid., 2.

8. Brock and Parker, *Proverbs of Ashes*, 165–215.

healing. Yet, I still fear that Brock and Parker's conflation of evil and patriarchy obscures something about the nature of evil.

In their thought, patriarchy was equated with dominance, and dominance was implicitly equated with authority. The result is that there can be no such thing as a benevolent patriarchy or benevolent authority; by its very nature patriarchy is domineering and malevolent. While this may feel true from the perspective of an abused child, it is not always true. Not every child is abused in a society in which men have most of the power and authority.

Let's ask it this way: Can a man who has authority over a woman use that authority for her good? Of course he can. In fact, it happens all of the time in families and workplaces in Western culture. I myself, as an elite man in a hierarchal workplace, have used my power to promote the careers and welfare of women who worked for me (or, in some cases, for whom I worked). Such power that I held, I used to enhance the responsibilities and freedom of subordinate women—that is to empower them, not simply paternalistically promote what I believed to be in their best interest. Nor am I alone; I have seen supervisors promote the interests of their employees, teachers promote the interests of their students, and fathers promote the interests of their daughters and wives. What are we to call this? Structurally, these examples are patriarchal because men hold power and authority over women. Certainly this power could be used to abuse or restrain these women, but in many, perhaps most, cases it is not. Rather, the power that these "benevolent" men hold is used to *serve, empower,* and *promote* the interests of subordinate women. The structure is patriarchal, but I fail to see how criticisms of dominance apply beyond the recognition of women's vulnerability. Brock and Parker failed to consider such positive cases.

A feminist might respond that by working in hierarchal systems, these "benevolent" men (as well as the women) support a system that ultimately harms more women than it helps and leaves all women vulnerable to abuse. I concede that this may be true, at least at times, but is it really possible not to have hierarchies or authorities? Would the world really be better without families or organizations that possess power and authority? If such things exist *at all*, then people will be vulnerable to abuse. In a world of *de facto* hierarchy, it seems to me that the best way to improve women's lives is for those with power to serve and empower those with less. In fact, authorities that act as servants seem to me to be an essential ingredient in communities of mutuality that feminists wish to see transform the world. Moreover, it is the vision of leadership advocated in the Christian Scriptures.[9]

My point is this: if, in patriarchal or hierarchal contexts where men have power over subordinate women, these men can and do serve and empower women, then we have a *good* state of affairs that resembles patriarchy without the "dominance" and abuse. In fact, it seems that this is exactly the good state of affairs that the Christian Scriptures promote. But if such a state of affairs is possible then feminists need to recognize a much more complicated relationship between Christianity and "patriarchy." I suggest that the images of God as a servantly king and a motherly Father will do far more to advance the welfare of women in a *de facto* "patriarchal" world than images that are unintelligible given the hierarchal context of both the ancient world and our present one. And, to be fair, feminists, including Brock, recognize an "ambivalence" in Scripture regarding "hierarchical powers."[10]

The ethical consequence of conflating authority with its abuse is the denial of value in the discipline of submission, by which I mean the willingness to yield one's desires for the sake of another. Of course, a victim of abuse ought *not* to submit to her abuser—not in the sense expressed above. Feminists are right to challenge an understanding of the discipline of submission that urges a person to more victimization at the hands of an abuser. But submission is a necessary companion of love and so will be required in any community of mutuality, whether marriage, family,

9. E.g., Matt 16:24–26; 18:1–5.

10. Brock, *Journeys by Heart*, 69. My reading of Scripture suggests that hierarchical powers are embraced and commended when they act as servants, that is, as God acts. Generally, Scripture casts great suspicion on human hierarchical powers that are usually self-aggrandizing. It is clear (rather than ambivalent) from Scripture that these worldly powers cannot save us.

office, church, or Sister Circle. If evangelicals are right to describe the Christian life of faith as the "glad surrender," then any theology that does away with submission will hinder rather than promote communities of mutuality.

An additional consequence of conflating authority and abuse is the downplaying of personal sin—that is, our complicity in the de-meaning of ourselves or others. Feminists are right to point out that, in some settings, sin and guilt have added to the pain and misery of women. This is certainly true in regards to (some) Christian attitudes toward prostitutes. In fact, Brock acknowledged the reality of sin and recognized that evil "leads us to sin" and that sin can contribute to evil. Moreover, she rightfully argued that sin is "something to be healed."[11] Traditional theologians should agree. Yet, she held back from recognizing the disobedience of sin and our culpability for it. I understand that she did this for good therapeutic motives—motives of grace and not condemnation. However, I fear that a refusal to face our own culpability for sin or acknowledge that it disrupts our relationship with God (i.e., that we are disobedient) does not promote our full healing.

The Scriptures teach that we ought to confess and repent of our sins.[12] Brock argued that "for all of our discussions of pride, evil, alienation, greed, racism, war, and so on, Christians have not been able to deal fully with the presence of evil in our own patriarchal hearts."[13] I take this to mean that, in part, our confession and repentance of sin has not brought about either full healing or redemption of the world from the evil of "patriarchy." (I find her use of "patriarchal hearts" here to be a frustratingly obscure signifier.) We must grant that liberation theologians have quite correctly shown that the evil in our world is more than our personal sin and that it needs to be confronted by more than personal confession and repentance. But Brock seemed to suggest that we should substitute confession and repentance with a "profound

11. Brock, *Journeys by Heart*, 7.

12. E.g. Matt 3:2, 17; John 8:11; Rom 6:15.

13. Brock, *Journeys by Heart*, 8.

acknowledgement of our primal interrelatedness."[14] While I certainly support greater acknowledgment of our interrelatedness, I fail to see how this is a more truthful and helpful response than confessing and repenting of our contribution to evil in the world.

In their *Proverbs of Ashes*, Brock and Parker discussed several destructive choices that they have made. Parker especially mourned her abortion, and she ably showed how her choice to destroy the life in her womb was interrelated to the choices of others. Parker blamed her theology of sacrifice for crippling her moral imagination, and thus limiting her "choice" regarding her abortion.[15] In so doing, her abortion became a destructive act (i.e., sin) against herself alone rather than a destructive act against both herself and her child. So while articulating clearly how her ideas and her husband conspired to trap her into making a destructive choice, she did not seem able to fully accept her own responsibility for the act. As she said, it was simply "the best [she] could do in the circumstances."[16]

I do not wish to downplay the crucial importance of circumstances, and for all I know, Parker did confess and repent of her destructive choice. My point is not to promote guilt regarding this specific act but to suggest that *full healing* requires us to acknowledge our own participation in the systems of evil in the world. This is certainly not to deny the existence or importance of de-meaning systems that constrain our choices, but how can we confront evil if we cannot even confront our own responsibility for it in our heart? So while we ought to do much more to oppose evil, it seems to me that we should do *no less* than confess and repent of our sin.[17]

Brock clearly wished the church was better than it was. Unfortunately, she was correct to point out how the church—or its members—have often abetted the evils of this world. Yet, the church is an easy target—it has such high standards that are so

14. Ibid.

15. Brock and Parker, *Proverbs of Ashes*, 23–26.

16. Ibid., 25.

17. Parker does acknowledge that "we are all trying to recover from living a lie" (ibid., 215), so it may be that I have not done justice to her position.

consistently unmet. This suggests to me that the internal demons are, in fact, far more difficult to overcome. If so, then Brock's criticism that the church has not done all it can to deal with the evil in its heart does not imply we should stop taking that evil in our heart seriously. Confession and repentance of sin help us to take the evil in our own hearts seriously.

A holistic view of evil requires acknowledging its power to constrain our choices as well as the contribution our choices make to its power. Criticisms of evangelicals for focusing solely on personal sin are not unmerited. Brock, Parker, and liberation theologians in general offer a much-needed and important corrective to the small horizons of many evangelicals. Nonetheless, in their focus on the evil powers of patriarchy, Brock and Parker downplayed the personal role that we make in contributing to the destruction of others. Confessing and repenting of sin is important for women—including victims and survivors of the sex trade—because women, too, have made destructive choices and turned away from God. Moreover, men sin against women and one of the first steps to overcoming evil is for the oppressor to confess and repent of his sin.

Christians have traditionally held that evil was, is, and will be defeated through the life, death, and resurrection of Jesus Christ. The Christian "'answer' to the 'problem of evil' is," as theologian Kenneth Surin wrote, "the hesitant, stammering bringing of this reconciling action to speech."[18] Given the mystery of Christ's work on the cross, our theology ought to reflect a good measure of humility. Yet, as we hesitate and stammer our way toward a theology of the atonement (and our consequent gratitude), we must acknowledge that some things we could say about the death and resurrection of Jesus are better than other things. Since the doctrine of atonement stands at the center of our Christian "answer" to the problem of evil and since Brock and Parker were primarily concerned with its soteriology in their works, we must now turn our attention to the work of Christ.

18. Surin, *Theology and the Problem of Evil*, 143.

Both Brock and Parker offered sustained criticisms of traditional Christian soteriology, especially in regards to the meaning of the cross. While they claimed that all traditional theories of atonement are unsatisfactory, Brock and Parker were most disturbed by the popular idea that Jesus had to die in order to satisfy the angry Father so as to turn away his wrath from humankind. Parker argued: "Do we really believe that God is appeased by cruelty, and wants nothing more than our obedience? It becomes imperative that we ask this question when we examine how theology sanctions human cruelty. If God is imagined as a fatherly torturer, earthly parents are also justified, perhaps even required, to teach through violence . . . The child or the spouse who believes that obedience is what God wants may put up with physical or sexual abuse in an effort to be a good Christian."[19] Parker knew from experience people who had extended their own victimization in order to be good Christians. Her criticism of the sacrificial view of atonement stemmed from her pastoral concern.

In her effort to formulate a feminist Christology, Brock similarly argued that the patriarchal family has thoroughly distorted our view of God. She took issue with an omnipotent father-god who "fosters dependence" as well as the abusive "parent-child fusion" that classical Trinitarian thought is said to reflect.[20] In regard to traditional understandings of atonement, she stated:

> Such doctrines of salvation reflect by analogy, I believe, images of the neglect of children or, even worse, child abuse, making it acceptable as divine behavior—cosmic child abuse, as it were. The father allows, or even inflicts, the death of his only perfect son. The emphasis is on the goodness and power of the father and the unworthiness and powerlessness of his children, so that the father's punishment is just, and children are to blame. While atonement doctrines emphasize the father's grace and forgiveness, making it seem as if he accepts all persons whole without the demand that they be good and free of

19. Brock and Parker, *Proverbs of Ashes*, 31.

20. Brock, *Journeys by Heart*, 54–55.

> sin, such acceptance is contingent upon the suffering of the one perfect child.[21]

Brock allowed that such a theology can produce graciousness in individuals. She contended, however, that these doctrines do nothing to reform the patriarchal model of the family and thus perpetuate abuse of children and wives. Suffering is thus "built into the social structures."[22]

I have already argued above that I find Brock and Parker's understanding of patriarchy and evil to be vague, unconvincing, and incomplete. Here, I want to take issue with their criticism of the traditional doctrine of atonement. But before I do, we need to acknowledge that their criticism is not groundless. For those that have been abused, especially at the hands of their fathers, seeing God the Father as a cosmic child-abuser makes sense, especially in light of sacrificial views of atonement. We should acknowledge that this critique does legitimately cast doubt on any view of the cross in which Jesus appeases an angry or bloodthirsty God, and our preaching ought to reflect the sensitivity to which Brock and Parker call us. Yet while I do not wish to deny these pastoral insights, I find Brock and Parker's treatment of traditional Christology problematic for two reasons. First, their argument seems to assume that the Christian God is a projection of our own patriarchal vision. Second, their simplification of the Christian doctrine of atonement into cosmic child-abuse is unscriptural, and thus an unfair representation of what Christianity has taught about the atonement.

Brock asserted that the image of God the Father derives from a "nostalgic longing" for the "nurturing, intimate father" that is "absent in patriarchal society."[23] Because this imagined divine father's love is "largely unreal," Christian thinkers have developed the "doctrines of divine *apatheia* and [. . .] the assertion that the

21. Ibid., 56.

22. Ibid., 57.

23. Ibid., 53.

highest love is agape, a love based on objective dispassion."[24] At its heart, Christian theology results from the misguided "nostalgia of abused children" who seek to "realize mutuality and interdependence" by "being subject to unilateral power."[25] Any reluctance to give up such nostalgia grows out of our lack of honesty "about [our] experiences in patriarchal society."[26] An honest evaluation of our nostalgia will reveal what is missing: "interdependence—the intimacy, respect, and love necessary to loving the whole and compassionate being that comes from connectedness."[27] Thus, Brock argued that the traditional understanding of God is ultimately a projection of the God we wished exist, given our experience of abuse. She advocated a radical reevaluation of God, Christ, and what it means to be saved.

In this way, her work bears some resemblance to the nineteenth-century liberal thinker Ludwig Feuerbach who argued that we projected our image of ourselves onto God. He wrote:

> Consciousness of God is self-consciousness, knowledge of God is self-knowledge. By his God thou knowest the man, and by the man his God; the two are identical. Whatever is God to a man, that is his heart and soul; and conversely, God is the manifested inward nature, the expressed self of a man. . . .
>
> . . . Hence the historical progress of religion consists in this: that what by an earlier religion was regarded as objective, is now recognised as subjective; that is, what was formerly contemplated and worshipped as God is now perceived to be something *human*. What was at first religion becomes at a later period idolatry; man is seen to have adored his own nature. Man has given objectivity to himself, but has not recognised the object as his own

24. Ibid.
25. Ibid., 54.
26. Ibid.
27. Ibid.

> nature: a later religion takes this forward step; every advance in religion is therefore a deeper self-knowledge.[28]

Brock and Parker, like Feuerbach, genuinely wish for progress in religion; for Brock and Parker, the desire is for a religion that envisions and promotes a world of mutuality and interdependence. The Trinity is too patriarchal, too ripe for misuse—it is, in fact, "unholy," as Brock put it.[29] Thus, they argued that traditional Christian doctrines must be replaced with feminist Christian ones.

Ironically, I find there is a certain patronizing quality in the implication that most of us have created a god of our own imagining and we would do better with the god that Brock imagined for us. I do not want to deny that there is no temptation to create our own gods after our own image—the Christian Scripture teaches that this is so—yet, Brock seemed to suggest that there really is nothing (or nothing much) *out there* with whom to relate. This seems to contradict the historical experiences of hundreds of millions of Christians (not to mention adherents to other faiths). Was the Trinity to whom Saint Patrick prayed day and night while a child-slave in Ireland a nostalgic patriarchal projection? If so, then why send Patrick back to Ireland to risk re-enslavement after having freed him?[30] Or how should we think of the millions of low-class Romans who first converted to Christianity in the first centuries? Did they replace their imagined gods with an improved imagined God? Or did they encounter a real presence, a power that healed their diseases or aided them in distress as their testimonies indicate?[31] Did my friend Leslie conjure up an imagined Jesus coming to rescue her on the day she decided to kill herself? Can we really credit an imagined, nostalgic projection with the

28. Feuerbach, *The Essence of Christianity*, 33.

29. Brock, *Journeys by Heart*, xii.

30. Patrick, *The Confession of St. Patrick*, stanzas 16–23.

31. See MacMullen, *Christianizing the Roman Empire*, 39–42. MacMullen concludes his discussion on the conversion of millions of Romans before Constantine: "The explicit record at important points fits badly with what are, to ourselves, entirely natural expectations. The record and the expectations I have tried to compare in this chapter; but we must, of course, favor the former."

successful growth of Christianity throughout the ages? Why the consistent testimony across time and cultures that Christians have encountered Jesus Christ risen from the dead?[32] Can Feuerbach really account for the persuasive power of Christianity? I belabor this point because it does not seem to me at all likely that we can explain the totality of the Christian experience if we believe in gods of our own imagination.[33]

Perhaps I have misread Brock and Parker; perhaps they do confess a transcendent God but merely emphasize divine immanence. If so, their vision of God as the cosmic child-abuser does not do justice to the testimony of Jesus and his followers found in Scripture. Jesus taught that his Father was eager to receive, heal, and save those who sought him. We, however, are not eager to seek God, and our refusal to do so endangers us, not because God is greedy for worship, but because our sin is destructive and God will one day make the world right.[34] Moreover, the Trinitarian images that Brock attacked as demonstrating a "fusion" similar to that between an abuser and victim[35] are better read as the foundation for all mutuality and interdependence. It is understandable why some victims of abuse might read the Scriptures cynically, but I do not see why we must accede to that interpretation. Abuse is so disruptive of healthy relationships that is seems far better for the church to read the Scriptures in a way that is faithful to the testimony recorded therein. The twentieth century saw a revival of interest in the Trinity and one of the most natural consequences is to understand the Trinity as the foundation for communities of mutuality, interdependence, and love—exactly the sort of communities that feminists want to advance.[36] Moreover, I do not see how Brock can claim Scripture for a feminist Christianity if she reads abuse *into* and *against* the natural reading of the text. It seems wiser to

32. See Robinson, *Can We Trust the New Testament?*, 127.

33. For a modern philosophical argument for the existence of God from religious experience, see Kwan, "The Argument from Religious Experience."

34. E.g. Matt 8:5–13, 18:10–20, 20:29–34, 22:1–14.

35. Brock, *Journeys by Heart*, 54.

36. See, for example, LaCugna, *God for Us*.

either embrace the Trinity as the source and goal of feminist theology or to reject the Scriptures and Christianity altogether.

Traditional Christian theology claims that through the death and resurrection of Jesus Christ, evil has been and will be defeated in the world. Brock and Parker claimed that this theology perpetuates the evils of patriarchy—especially child abuse—in the world today. Because Brock and Parker seemed to believe that God is, ultimately, a projection of our nostalgic wishes, rather than a real being we encounter, they were able to read into and against Scripture an image of an angry father-god who abuses his passive sacrificial son. While their analysis is certainly useful pastorally, I do not think that they have succeeded in defeating the traditional views of the atonement. In order to make their claims, they must reject the testimony of hundreds of millions of Christians across time and cultures. This seems a very high price to pay in order to be pastorally sensitive to the abused within our pews, especially since many other grieving people—including victims of abuse such as my friend Leslie—have found comfort and some measure of healing in a relationship with the suffering and living Christ of Scripture and tradition.[37]

I have examined Brock and Parker's christological criticisms because, for the Christian, Jesus Christ is the final "answer" we have to the "problem" of evil. We claim that, through Christ's death and resurrection, our lives can be given meaning despite the existence of evil in the world. If evil de-means us, through Christ, our lives can be made whole again. Brock and Parker disagree. I want to turn attention to their constructive counter-proposal. How might we defeat evil, if Christ has not done it?

In the works of Brock and Parker, Jesus Christ does not save us, though he does help point the way. According to Brock, we are saved by "erotic power," which she defined, following Haunani-Kay Trask, as "the 'life-force,' the unique human energy which springs from the desire for existence with meaning, for a consciousness

37. See also Ilibagiza, *Left to Tell*; Lewis, *A Grief Observed*; Wolterstorff, *Lament for a Son*. I do not wish to minimize the tragic quality of evil or abuse. Many others have lost faith.

informed by feeling, for experience that integrates the sensual and the rational, the spiritual and the political. In the feminist vision, Eros is both love *and* power."[38]

This power, repressed by patriarchy, is not primarily about cause and effect, but about the interrelatedness of our very being. It "involves the whole person in relationships of self-awareness, vulnerability, openness, and caring."[39] It is also the source of Jesus' power to love others—a source rooted in the communities that loved and reared him. Jesus' own work is not that of the singular hero, but that of the "erotic power within the Christa/Community."[40] In fact, this erotic power is the essential divine energy at work healing broken-heartedness.

In this view, of course, the crucifixion of Jesus was tragic because it was entirely unnecessary.[41] Erotic power grows from *life*, not death. To claim that his death was good is to say that "state terrorism is a good thing, that torture and murder are the will of God."[42] The resurrection was not an objective raising of Christ from the dead, but the community's affirmation of the erotic power within the community—a community that would survive Jesus' death because they refused to let "go of their relationships to each other." Jesus is "brought back," not by the power of God, but by the community's "memory and visionary-ecstatic image of resurrection."[43]

This erotic power felt in each other through the tragedy of Jesus' death and remembered through their "visionary-ecstatic image of resurrection" is sufficient to ground the "call to wholehearted discipleship."[44] The "Christa/Community" perpetuates erotic power in the world. Remembering Jesus, we become Christ as we "stand in solidarity with all who suffer" and "confront and

38. Brock, *Journeys by Heart*, 25, citing Trask.

39. Brock, *Journeys by Heart*, 26.

40. Ibid., 66–67.

41. Ibid., 93.

42. Brock and Parker, *Proverbs of Ashes*, 49.

43. Brock, *Journeys by Heart*, 100.

44. Ibid., 99.

feel deeply the tragic loss of all who suffer and die." In this way, the broken-hearted may be healed.[45]

I believe this re-visioning of Christianity to be untenable. First, it suggests that ultimately we save ourselves, a suggestion I believe to be unrealistic. Second, it depends on an imaginary history. Third, it does nothing about the de-meaning quality of death. And fourth, it deprives people of an eschatological hope necessary for sustained ethical commitment. If the Christian revelation is true, I contend that the traditional interpretations of Christ's life, death, and resurrection to be a far superior response to the problem of evil and de-meaning.

I find Brock's articulation of erotic power to be frustratingly ephemeral, though perhaps this reveals my own limitations of understanding. I find unconvincing the idea that this "divine" energy is fundamentally derived from human interrelatedness. This erotic power comes not from the living God, but from our being-in-relationship. If so, then it will really be up to us to increase its influence in the world. I appreciate the urgency that lends to ethics of liberation, but, if true, I am highly dubious humanity will ever be successful at creating a world of whole-hearted love without divine intervention. It seems that history shows us that we, as a species, can barely find the internal erotic power to keep civilization from plunging into barbarism and destruction. Though I do acknowledge that innate human goodness can resist evil to an extent, I am more sympathetic to the scriptural notion that it is God's grace that is responsible for the survival of humankind to date, not our own erotic power. Perhaps my first objection is fundamentally an intuition: I simply do not *feel* that we can make ourselves better without divine aid. Those who do not share my intuition may find Brock more convincing.

Brock's contention that the Christa/Community raised Jesus from the dead in their memory and through an ecstatic vision runs counter to all scriptural testimony. The confession of Christ's death and resurrection found in 1 Corinthians 15:3–5 is widely agreed to come from the very early church. The testimony found

45. Ibid., 103–4.

in the Gospels all points to the belief that the earliest community did not simply "remember" Jesus or have an "ecstatic vision" of him, but believed that he had been brought back to life by God. Moreover the hypothesis that a demoralized community could have had such detailed group visionary experiences (that they all interpreted as real rather than as a dream or spiritual vision) is simply unbelievable. No modern psychological theory could explain such an event.[46] It is certainly possible to reject the resurrection as ahistorical, but it seems far safer simply to reject the Scriptures altogether. To argue that, despite its consistent testimony otherwise, the Scriptures really do not mean Jesus rose from the dead does injustice to the text and the original authors. Since Brock was unwilling to call the authors liars, she must instead patronize them. Her assumption that no physical resurrection took place is not based on the actual historical testimony, but, in all likelihood, on her materialistic assumptions. The authors of Scripture are united in their testimony that Jesus was raised by the power of the living God. Thus, there is no *historical* basis for her interpretation of erotic power in the earliest Christian community; she has simply imagined it.

If evil is, as I have suggested, de-meaning, then the greatest evil is death. As I have argued in earlier chapters, in this world, death appears to devour all meaning. Existentially, we struggle to find meaning in the deaths of those whom we love, but these struggles pale in comparison to efforts to seek meaning in events of great death such as the Holocaust or Rwandan genocide. Moreover, modern science teaches that one day the earth will become inhospitable to life. And after the earth, the solar system, and eventually the entire universe will fade into darkness. Death will devour us all. Once no one is left to remember, then the universe will have been de-meaned, unless, of course, Jesus Christ *was* resurrected. While Brock and Parker's efforts to promote hope in the face of the final death and de-meaning are commendable, they seem misplaced. If love really is grounded in human interrelatedness, then love is doomed.

46. McGrew and McGrew, "The Argument from Miracles," 604, 623.

Because Brock and Parker deny the reality of the resurrection, their final hope—or eschatology—is significantly constrained. It does seem that Brock and Parker believe in something after this life, but their eschatological hope is for a post-patriarchal future of mutuality and love. I agree that mutuality and love are certainly things to work for, but without the resurrection, or divine assistance for that matter, this eschatological hope seems rather far-fetched. The Christian who believes that we will all be resurrected knows that in the end what we do here *really matters*. But if my great goal is a post-patriarchal world that is so far in the future as to be almost unimaginable, why spend my life for its sake? I do not see how a vision of erotic power can ground the hope necessary to sustain lifelong solidarity with the oppressed. But, if Christ suffered, died, and rose again, then I can be assured that my efforts to love and stand beside others—empowered by the Holy Spirit—are worth it.

Finally, Brock and Parker can only offer mutual relationship to the broken-hearted. Of course, I agree that we *must* create communities of mutuality, grace, and healing—that this is part of our Christian commitment. But because Brock does not appear to believe that the divine is anything beyond a human life-force, she cannot offer anything more. For all of the church's sins, hypocrisies, and mistakes, surely our greatest treasure is our relationship with the living Triune God. The testimonies of millions affirm this. Today, Christianity is spreading rapidly in parts of the world where people live in great material want and daily face evil that would de-mean their lives.[47] The message that drives the growth of the Christian religion is that one may know God. I confess I long for deep communities of mutuality and love, but I also long for the love of God. Humanity is not enough. If, in the person of Jesus Christ, we really have encountered God with us, then feminist theologians do the oppressed and abused a disservice by denying them a relationship with this God.

I have found significant fault with the Christian feminist theology of Rita Nakashima Brock and Rebecca Parker. While I

47. Jenkins, *The Next Christendom*.

believe that evangelicals have much to learn from them and other feminist and liberation theologians, I have argued that Brock and Parker failed to take evil seriously enough. This is evident by a downplaying of individual human contributions to evil (i.e., sin) as well as a re-visioned Christology that ultimately posits we can save ourselves. While I commend their deep and good desire to stand with the oppressed, I maintain that they withhold important resources to sustain the struggle for the reign of God. The poor, abused, and oppressed need divine aid and an eschatological hope that will ground their struggle for healing and meaning. Most of all we need a relationship with the living God, not an imagined substitute. The life, death, and resurrection of Jesus Christ is good news—especially for the poor, abused, and oppressed of the earth.

# 5

# Evil and the Christian Mission to Prostitutes

In writing about evil and the challenges it poses to Christians, atheists, and feminists, I have frequently referred to the sex trade as an example of de-meaning and horrendous evil. It should be evident from these discussions that differing understandings of evil have different ethical consequences. In this final chapter, I intend to consider some of these ethical consequences for both Christians engaged in the mission to prostitutes and opponents of this mission who have a very different understanding of evil and salvation. While we Christians have some things to learn from others with different perspectives, I hope to show that the Christian narrative of salvation takes evil more seriously and offers more hope for healing then the narrative proposed by our critics.

In 2009, I attended the International Christian Alliance on Prostitution's regional conference in Costa Rica. My friends and I had just begun modest efforts to help prostitutes in Jarabacoa, our mountain town of 60,000 or so in the Dominican Republic. At the conference, Lauran Bethell, a key leader in the Alliance, told us that the Holy Spirit was raising up people all over the world to reach out to women, children, and men in prostitution. Like many others in the Christian mission to prostitutes, my own involvement is not the result of a logical or efficient application of my skill set to a specific problem, but rather my faltering attempt to respond to the invitation to join Jesus Christ in his mission to a people that is very precious to him.

While the Christian mission to prostitutes began with Jesus Christ himself, globalization has lent a new urgency to the invitation. The "flattening" of the world, as Thomas L. Friedman called it,[1] has not only benefitted productive commerce, but it has also allowed criminal networks to operate with greater freedom and viciousness. Trafficking in drugs, weapons, and humans is not only interrelated globally, but has deep ties to licit commerce as well. For most people, crime, not terrorism, poses a greater threat to their livelihood and very lives.[2] Mexico offers an especially clear example of the power of organized crime where drug cartels not infrequently send "heavily armed battalions to attack police stations and [assassinate] police officers, government officials and journalists."[3] This violence takes its toll on Mexican society, encouraging a culture where, as Mexican novelist Mario Bellatin said, "It's as if the whole country were made up of people who rent and people who are rented, as if one half of society has contracted the other to carry out the role of mutilated corpse, hit man, corrupt official or missing woman."[4] The church ought to be concerned about the increasing power of organized crime.

I have a friend in Mexico who helps girls leave prostitution and is convinced that eventually the mafia will come for him and kill him. Most Western Christian protest against "worldly powers" has been directed against governments, and more recently, large corporations, and with merit. Western Christians are not yet used to thinking of organized crime as one of the "powers" arrayed against the kingdom of God, but soon may be. I propose that the sex trade represents one of the great evils of our age—one

1. Friedman, *The World is Flat.*

2. Glenny, *McMafia*; McGill, *Human Traffic.*

3. O'Neil, "The Real War in Mexico," 63.

4. Bellatin, "Human Currency in Mexico's Drug Trade."

of the "spiritual forces of evil" with which we struggle.[5] For many centuries, Christians have tried to help those caught within the sex trade and some within the church continue to confront this evil and offer hope and healing to the many people broken and de-meaned by its power. It is important for the whole church to support this crucial effort.

But while the church has always had a mission to proclaim healing for prostitutes, Christians are not the only ones with a narrative of salvation. Some within the secular Western academy also have a story of salvation that is at odds with the Christian story. In this chapter, I have set myself two tasks: first, to summarize and criticize the secular academy's "redefinitional" narrative of salvation for prostitutes and, second, to highlight some emphases of the Christian salvation narrative that the church must remember in its mission to prostitutes.

As I argued in the first chapter, one function of evil is to constrict freedom. Of course no one is perfectly free—we are all constrained by our contexts. But a free person is able to choose among various life-affirming activities. Evil limits these options. Addictions to harmful substances, for example, are evil because it becomes more and more difficult for a person to make life-affirming choices. In other evil systems—such as war, genocide, or persecution—a person's only life-affirming choice may mean death for oneself or others. Forces that constrict freedom for women, men, and children in the sex trade may include social stigma, poverty and lack of opportunities, concern for safety and care of children or other family members, poor coping skills resulting from past trauma, drug or alcohol addiction, fear of harm, and actual harm—beatings, rape, torture—should one fail to obey one's controller, and despair. Typically we call someone whose freedom is so constricted a *victim*, a word that is supposed to connote the moral condemnation of the constricting circumstances and the moral innocence of the victim. Moreover, victimhood creates certain moral obligations for other third parties—the obligation to help or to rescue. We shall see, however, that the ideas of *victim*

5. Eph 6:12.

and *rescue* are part of the contested salvation narratives surrounding prostitution.

Evil is the great test of every worldview. Every salvation narrative must help us both take the power of evil seriously and give us hope that evil can and will be defeated.[6] Any salvation story that fails in either of these tasks is not salvation at all. In fact, only a salvation story that takes evil with utmost seriousness can defeat it. This is exactly what the Christian gospel does. Only Christ's own death can overcome evil and death through his resurrection that envelops us in a new creation and a new life. Twenty centuries of theological reflection have not quite enabled us to say exactly *how* God saves, but the church nonetheless continues to proclaim and to experience God's salvation.

Christians are not the only ones with a mission to prostitutes. Many Hindus, Buddhists, communists, and post-Christians are deeply concerned about women in prostitution and take action to help them. For example, Anuradha Koirala, a Hindu, and her group Maiti Nepal "rescue and rehabilitate" victims and survivors of the sex trade and trafficking in Nepal and India.[7] In the West, the most vocal post-Christian critics of the sex trade are feminists. In fact, Christians share with these other opponents of prostitution—especially post-Christian feminists—a similar salvation narrative. Both Christians and feminists believe that the objectification of women and others in prostitution is de-meaning. Both understand that women in prostitution have very limited options and are often enslaved. Both acknowledge that most, if not all, prostitutes do not deserve moral condemnation, but rather our help. Yet post-Christian feminists are extremely wary of Christian churches, and look to form alliances with other non-Christian organizations that typically fall along the political Left, though in this they are often disappointed.[8]

Despite many shared values and beliefs, the Christian salvation narrative is different from the narrative proclaimed by

6. Walls, "Outrageous Evil."

7. Ruffins, "Rescuing Girls from Sex Slavery."

8. See, for example, Clarke, "Prostitution for Everyone," 157.

others seeking to help prostitutes. The most important difference, of course, is that Christians proclaim the saving power of Jesus Christ. Yet, in many ways the mission to prostitutes of Christians and others can offer mutual support because their goals overlap. But there is another salvation narrative that is hostile to all of these efforts, whether motivated by religious or feminist concerns. It is this alternative and hostile narrative that I wish to consider here.

This alternative narrative is a product of the Western academy and looks to empower prostitutes by redefining prostitution as *sex work*, thereby raising sex worker's social status and dignifying them with protections other workers receive. Because of its emphasis on *redefining* sex work, I will call this alternative narrative the "redefinitional narrative." At its heart, the redefinitional narrative rejects the idea that (most) prostitutes are *victims* in need of *rescue*. What sex workers do need are safer and freer working conditions as well as social respect. The redefinitional narrative rests on three ideas: (1) that prostitution is a kind of work, (2) that sex work is (usually) chosen, and (3) that we ought to listen to the voices of sex workers and support their working goals, rather than "rescue" them. Advocates for this narrative, such as Cheryl Overs of the Network of Sex Work Projects, desire the decriminalization and legalization of all aspects of prostitution.[9]

The redefinitional strategy begins by redefining prostitution as sex work. Kamala Kempadoo, a leading scholar of prostitution, followed Than-Dam Troung in arguing that prostitution is a form of work. Troung and Kempadoo defined work as "the way in which basic needs are met and human life produced and reproduced." Because sex fulfills basic human needs for pleasure and procreation, it is therefore work. Moreover, all work involves specific parts of the body, just as sexual labor does. Finally, sexual labor is socially constructed—there is no one "right" way to go about it. Kempadoo argued that "sexual labor has been organized for the re-creation and replenishment of human and social life" through "wet-nursing, temple prostitution, 'breeding' under

9. Doezema, "International Activism," 208. Overs even seeks the decriminalization of child prostitution.

slavery, surrogate child-bearing, donor sex, commercial sex and biological reproduction."[10] Because commercial sex is a form of work it ought to be divorced from the idea that sex and love *ought* to be conjoined. In fact, any such moral position represents an "essentialist cultural interpretation . . . imposed upon" the sex worker.[11] Many within the sex industry, even children, are able to distinguish between sex as work and sex as an expression of affection; thus, we should respect this distinction.[12] Recognizing sexual labor for what it is will allow women to make gains for equality in an industry that currently privileges men as well as giving all sex workers the protections that normally apply for workplaces.

Legitimizing sex work also requires us to acknowledge the agency of sex workers themselves. To this end, sex worker advocates emphasize and respect the choices of sex workers. Kempadoo, following scholars Judith Kegan Gardiner and Wendy Chapkis, understood the recognition of women's agency to be essential for feminist thought and practice.[13] She and Cheryl Overs chastised other feminists who fail to applaud those sex workers who seek to reform the sex industry rather than abolish it. These feminists are "anti-sex" moralists and "puritans" producing "drivel about sexual slavery."[14] That is, Kempadoo and her colleagues accused anti-prostitution feminists of being nearly identical to the Christian mission to prostitutes, though anti-prostitution feminists deny this.[15] The essence of the critique is that anti-prostitution feminists (and Christians, assumedly) continue to see sex workers as objects ("victims") and not human agents.[16] Redefining and legitimizing sex work ought to be integral to the feminist agenda.

10. Kempadoo, "Introduction: Globalizing Sex Workers Rights," 4.

11. Ibid., 5.

12. Ibid., 5, 7. See also Montgomery, "Children, Prostitution, and Identity."

13. Kempadoo, "Introduction: Globalizing Sex Workers Rights," 9; Gardiner, *Provoking Agents*, 9; Chapkis, *Live Sex Acts*, 29–30.

14. Doezema, "International Activism," 206.

15. For example, see Clarke, "Prostitution for Everyone," 191.

16. Kempadoo, "Introduction: Globalizing Sex Workers Rights," 9.

As part of their effort to show that sex workers freely choose their work, redefinitional advocates challenge prevailing assumptions about the "forced" nature of prostitution. Australian researcher and sex worker Alison Murray suggested that very little work in the sex trade involves trafficking, slavery, or child prostitution. Rather these terms are used by "extremists" such as the (secular, feminist) Coalition against Trafficking in Women (CATW) in their efforts to win support for ending the trade.[17] Murray acknowledged that when sex workers have been forced into the trade, they ought to be helped, but she wanted "abolitionists" to hear "that most sex workers . . . do their job willingly and do very well out of it relative to other occupations."[18] Generally, sex worker organizations and their allies have succeeded in differentiating between voluntary and forced prostitution; many government agencies and non-governmental organizations now recognize this difference. Yet, drawing distinctions between voluntary and forced prostitution can be difficult. For example, a woman may be forced into prostitution initially, but remain in it voluntarily, and some women are trafficked overseas knowing that they will work as prostitutes. Distinguishing between voluntary and forced prostitution also encourages the assumption that Western sex workers have agency while sex workers in developing nations do not. But the most pressing difficulty the distinction poses for sex worker advocates is that it divides prostitutes into the guilty and innocent. Society helps those deemed innocent, but ignores or damns the guilty.[19]

The idea that prostitution, if consensual, is a "victimless" crime is popular. Whenever anti-prostitution advocates or officials try to argue that the sex trade demeans women, a well-educated and self-confident prostitute can be found to cast doubt on these arguments, as happened in 2010 on Fox's *John Stossel Show*.[20] The

17. Murray, "Debt-Bondage and Trafficking," 52.

18. Ibid., 62.

19. Doezema, "Forced to Choose," 37, 41–47; Sandy, "Just Choices."

20. Wendy Murphy and Kat Smith, interview by John Stossel, *The John Stossel Show*, Fox Business News, March 4, 2010, http://www.iswface.org/

redefinitional narrative has had some success in marginalizing anti-prostitution feminists from American policy debates. But, during his administration, George W. Bush encouraged policies directed toward reducing (and ultimately eradicating) prostitution as a part of the United States's efforts against human trafficking.[21] These efforts reflected both evangelical and feminist fears about the normalization of prostitution in society.[22]

The final pillar on which the redefinitional narrative stands is the moral imperative to acquiesce to what sex workers themselves want—or at least what the advocates of this narrative say they want. The imperative has several sources. First, since the late 1960s, American feminist theory has been deeply concerned with listening to all women's voices. Both black and lesbian feminists offered sharp criticisms of traditional white and "heterosexist" feminism; criticisms white feminists have accepted.[23] Kempadoo, Doezema, Murray, and other sex worker advocates want "conventional feminists" to listen to the voices of sex workers, rather than pass moral judgments on them. Murray put it this way: "Support of sex workers' rights is part of a larger post-modern challenge to conventional feminism, which allows for a cacophony of voices and refuses the binary dichotomy in which all women are constituted as 'other.' Feminism which fails to overcome binary oppositions ends up supporting the status quo, impoverishing women and aligning with right-wing fundamentalism and a discourse which has its genesis in homophobia."[24]

According to Murray and others, feminism betrays its roots when it pronounces what is best for the "other." The moral imperative is further reinforced by a commitment to cultural relativity. Telling sex workers that prostituting themselves is bad is yet another way elites exercise power over the marginalized. Even distinguishing between relatively well-to-do prostitutes in the West and

(accessed 1 May 2010).

21. DeStefano, *The War on Human Trafficking*, 110–17.

22. Weitzer, "The Movement to Criminalize Sex Work," 64.

23. Donovan, *Feminist Theory*, 169–82.

24. Murray, "Debt-Bondage and Trafficking," 52.

desperately poor prostitutes in the developing world exemplifies a colonial mentality. Consequently, sex worker advocates applaud sex worker organizations in the developing world. Finally, to suggest that consensual sex has limits is inherently oppressive. On what philosophical grounds can we forbid consensual commercial sex but retain the right to every other kind of consensual sex? Asking us to discipline ourselves in this one respect is inconsistent.

The end result is that sex worker advocates reject both the idea of victimhood and the need for "rescue." Instead, sex workers need to stand up for their own right to work as they desire (in the trade or out of it), and we ought to offer our resources to help them. While being a victim might remove the moral stigma of prostitution, it adds the moral stigma of passivity as well as ensuring that those who choose sex work will continue to suffer ostracism. Accordingly, no moral judgments ought to be made about sex workers at all; moral judgment harms, de-means, and separates the sex worker from society. Thus, in the redefinitional narrative, salvation comes from letting sex workers work in safe environments, free of abuse, shame, or guilt.

While sex worker advocates have primarily attacked anti-prostitution feminists,[25] one scholar has specifically criticized the Christian mission to prostitutes in Thailand from the redefinitional perspective. Darla Y. Schumm analyzed the Christian missionary response to prostitution in Thailand in her 2002 doctoral dissertation. She focused on four different mission organizations working directly with prostitutes: the Fatima Center, a Catholic refuge run by the Good Shepherd Sisters; New Life Center, a residential project for tribal girls whose first director was Lauran Bethell (now based in Amsterdam); Rahab Ministries, a holistic mission to prostitutes founded by the late Patricia Green (before her death with Alabaster Jar, a ministry to prostitutes in Berlin); and Empower, a secular advocacy organization co-founded with Mennonite Max Ediger (now in Hanoi). She found that the Christian missions practiced

25. See, for example, Doezema, "Ouch! Western Feminists' 'Wounded Attachment.'"

a variety of strategies, including prevention, conversion, rescue, rehabilitation, education, and empowerment.[26]

Schumm had two basic criticisms of the Christian mission to prostitutes in Thailand. First, she believed most of them to be "Orientalist," by which she means they believe Western Christian culture to be superior to Thai culture. For example, she declared that "Rahab most obviously promotes the belief that, via Christianity, the West has a responsibility to lead Asia into modernity and that the cultures of the Orient are therefore inferior to Western culture."[27] Even when missions try to contextualize Christianity in the local culture, they still "maintain that Christianity should be spread throughout the world, which implies that non-Christian religions are inferior and should be replaced by Christianity."[28] Schumm made it clear that she agrees with the Fourteenth Dalai Lama's suggestion that "it is best for people to adhere to the religious tradition of their upbringing" and "that all religious traditions have value and worth." She did recognize that Christians would need to re-examine what it means to be a Christian missionary if they "embraced this one simple truth that the Dalai Lama asserts."[29] Of course, her hope that Christians would follow the suggestions of the Buddhist Dalai Lama rather than the commands of Christ betrays another sort of cultural imperialism, a hypocrisy about which she seems oblivious.

More helpful, perhaps, was her observation regarding the continued difficulties in contextualizing the gospel for Thai culture. This is not a new problem. For example, Kosuke Koyama, a Japanese Christian missionary to Thailand, described how "noisy" the Christian gospel seemed to Thai Buddhists and how disturbing was God's wrath in a culture that valued tranquility.[30] Certainly, these and other aspects of the faith were and are stumbling blocks for Thais. But by accusing the missionaries of

26. Schumm, "The Self-Understanding," 159.

27. Ibid., 218.

28. Ibid., 219.

29. Ibid., 220.

30. Koyama, *Waterbuffalo Theology*, 95–96, 225–26.

Orientalism, Schumm actually obscured rather than clarified the Christian missionaries' *self*-understanding—her purported goal. First, she completely overlooked the tension between Christianity and the West and instead conflated the two. That both Bethell and Green worked with prostitutes in Europe by applying lessons learned from their experiences in Thailand suggests a more nuanced relationship between Christianity, the West, and Thailand. Moreover, Schumm failed to factor in the culture of prostitution, though she did claim to recognize the prostitute to be the "other of the other." But Christian missionaries to prostitutes such as Green are very aware of the cultural barriers—not only between the West and the local culture, but between the local culture and prostitute cultures.[31] Of course, the Christian missionaries do believe that women and children can have a better life outside of the sex trade, and, in a sense, this means they believe that prostitution culture is inferior to their own; yet, even Schumm agrees that the sex trade in Thailand is a "serious social problem."[32] Third, whereas Schumm seemed unimpressed with the friendship evangelism of the Christian missionaries, I know of no better way to overcome attitudes of cultural superiority than through friendship. In good friendships, all parties change and grow. As the Anglican clergyman from India, V. S. Azariah, proclaimed to the 1910 World Missionary Conference in Edinburgh, the people of India needed more than good works and heroic labor from Western missionaries: "We also ask for *love*. Give us FRIENDS!"[33] Christian missionaries can only share *who they are*. To expect Western missionaries to be something they are not is to diminish the possibility of true friendship and intercultural dialogue. And while Schumm did find some signs of condescension among Western missionaries, her study did not suggest that this attitude was prevalent among them. Ultimately it seems that Schumm was criticizing the Western missionaries for being *Western* and *missionaries*—that is, for thinking they have found something worth sharing with others. Schumm acknowl-

31. Patricia Green, email to author, 17 June 2009.

32. Schumm, "The Self-Understanding," 114.

33. Azariah, "The Problem of Co-operation," 315.

edged that the modern sex trade in Thailand is, in part, a Western creation, but it is the Western Christian efforts to redress the trade that are imperialistic![34] While Christian missionaries to prostitutes can no doubt be patronizing, ultimately, Schumm's criticisms seem unjustified. Schumm, too, is a Westerner with a Western plan to alleviate the sufferings of sex workers in the Western-sponsored Thai sex trade, and, unlike the missionaries she encountered there, she does not actually know any Thai prostitutes.[35]

Schumm also chided the Christian mission to prostitutes for not accepting the redefinitional salvation narrative. More specifically, she argued that for any mission to be effective, its work must include situational, structural, and redefinitional approaches to mitigating the problems of prostitution. Generally, Schumm credited the missions with providing situational assistance for some women, though she sees these as "'band aids' to deeper problems."[36] She was not as positive toward the missions' structural efforts to address the sex trade and believed these to be ineffective precisely "because . . . their adherence to a Western Christian perspective" keeps them from engaging "in the deep structural critiques and transformations necessary to realize true economic and legal reform or the radically altering cultural empowerment of Thai women."[37] Of course, the missions would no doubt like to see Thailand and the global sex trade radically transformed by Christianity, but I suspect that is not the sort of transformation Schumm believes is feasible.

34 Schumm, "The Self-Understanding," 41–43, 220.

35. Ibid., 2. Schumm: "While I argue throughout the dissertation that the most effective response to prostitution in Thailand must take the necessary step of incorporating the voices of Thai prostitutes, this study does not ultimately take that step. The primary task of this study is to assess the efficacy of the Christian missionary response to prostitution in Thailand and to demonstrate the necessity and create the space for the voices of Thai prostitutes. Nevertheless, I must be clear in stating that I recognize the seeming contradiction between my assertions and the focus of the dissertation, and that I do not intend to repeat the patterns of Orientalism I critique by not including the voices of Thai prostitutes."

36. Ibid., 231.

37. Ibid., 233.

Finally, Schumm, not surprisingly, found the missions opposed to the legitimization of prostitution. Only Empower advocates "that sex work is real work," but because Empower is now a secular organization, Schumm dismissed its relevance in her evaluation.[38] Schumm contended that "moral reasoning about sex work and sex workers must go beyond ethical concerns regarding the sexual immorality of prostitution to an expanded social ethical concern that stresses the empowerment of the personhood of Thai prostitutes and acts to improve the working conditions and human rights of Thai sex workers."[39] Because the Christian missions see the sex trade as evil and believe "that the majority of Thai prostitutes are coerced into the sex industry," they fail to participate in a salvation story that would make the sex trade a safer place to work.[40] That is to say, they are not really helping Thai prostitutes.

Sex worker advocates and critics of the Christian and feminist missions to prostitutes have done some thoughtful analysis from which we may learn. They are certainly right to warn about the danger in treating prostitutes as objects without a voice of their own. Not every prostitute wants to leave prostitution. In fact, prostitution is an exceedingly complex phenomenon that resists generalizations. One way anti-prostitution activists may objectify prostitutes is by focusing on the most horrendous stories in trying to gain sympathy for the cause. We are all fascinated by other people's pain, but, unless we actually do something to help others, stories of sexual slavery become a sort of perverse entertainment. We must be careful that we do not encourage a sort of Christian voyeurism that further victimizes real people.

Even those who do not advocate the normalization of sex work caution us against the widespread use of the word "rescue" for Christian efforts against human trafficking. "Rescue" implies a power differential between the rescuer and rescuee—and is frequently used to glorify the rescuer at the expense of the person being rescued. Moreover, "rescue" can imply a rather straightforward

38. Ibid., 235–36.

39. Ibid., 234–35.

40. Ibid., 235.

process of removal that defies the complexities of the sex trade. The word "rescue" is not used in related fields that help victims and survivors of domestic violence or sexual abuse.[41] Those who participate in the Christian mission to prostitutes need to be aware how using the word "rescue" may actually undermine efforts to help those in prostitution.

Another danger revealed by sex worker advocates is an over-reliance on legal remedies and a carelessness of thought regarding how the law promotes or limits the human rights of prostitutes as well as their ability to leave the trade. New Zealand decriminalized prostitution in 2003 and found in its 2008 review of the law that, though safety concerns persisted, most prostitutes felt safer and were more likely to report abuse to the police. The number of prostitutes did not increase.[42] By decriminalizing prostitution, New Zealand hoped to keep prostitution from going underground, and thus make it easier to help prostitutes leave the trade as well as improve working conditions for those women who remained in it. So far this approach seems to be having the desired effect, though the review committee reported "little dedicated support for those wishing to exit the sex industry."[43] Such a legal regime might make it easier for Christian missions to prostitutes to reach out to prostitutes, and so it possesses some advantages. Rather than simply asserting that decriminalization or legalization of prostitution is always harmful to prostitutes or society, Christians and feminists should give more careful thought to how the law might serve the mission to protect those in the trade and assist those who wish to leave it. One area of great concern is how modern technology and legal repression have moved prostitution indoors, especially in Europe and America, making it much more difficult for others to reach or befriend prostitutes.[44] Closed-door prostitution also removes it from the public eye, allowing polite society to pretend it does not exist. This may not be the direction we want

41. Owens-Bullard, "Take off the cape."

42. New Zealand Prostitution Law Review Committee, *Report*, 13–14.

43. Ibid., 15.

44. Bernstein, *Temporarily Yours.*

to move. Prohibition has not made prostitution unthinkable; perhaps creative interim decriminalization measures would be useful in both reducing harm in the sex trade and creating more spaces for missions to prostitutes to help women leave the trade and ultimately make prostitution unthinkable.

Despite these and other helpful criticisms and warnings, the fundamental vision of the redefinitional salvation story is nonetheless deeply flawed, failing to take evil seriously or give those opposing evil the courage they need to persevere against it.

As I described earlier, when I was visiting a friend who is working against the sex trade in Mexico, he took me into a brothel to show me what we were up against. The brothel was hidden away and secured behind locked doors. My friend told the woman at the desk that we were here for my bachelor party. Three somewhat skeptical adult women came out and posed for us in their clothes. Embarrassed and unable to even look at the women, I realized what it meant to buy someone—and shuddered in horror for what it must mean to sell oneself. Those women expected me to look at them as *things*, not as persons—to choose one (or more) of them to use. The expectation—the fundamental assumption—of prostitution is that I can buy someone for my own gratification. In order to purchase sex, the customer must de-mean the prostitute. Moreover, when a customer de-means a prostitute, he also de-means himself. Our own humanity—our own meaning—can never be enhanced by de-meaning someone else. Finally, the prostitute correspondingly sees the customer as a means to an end—and, in effect, de-means him as well. Prostitution is *essentially* de-meaning and always will be. The de-meaning character of prostitution makes it evil. This is why redefining prostitution as sex work fails to save anyone. Calling prostitution "sex work" does not change its de-meaning character.

While decriminalization might very well be advantageous for both prostitutes and the Christian missions to them, at least in some contexts, the *legitimization* of prostitution is harmful. Legitimization comes when elites within society interpret prostitution as a positive or neutral activity, and it seems to be the desired goal of sex worker advocacy. The basic idea supposes that, if consumers and bystanders thought of prostitutes as another type of professional service worker, then prostitutes would accrue more respect and self-respect. However, since prostitution is inherently de-meaning, this is simply not possible. One cannot disrespect a person by buying them for one's own gratification and at the same time respect them. Instead, legitimization makes it morally permissible for people to buy sex and thus de-mean people. It is not healthy for the society or the individuals involved.

Sex worker advocates believe that the buying and selling of sex is like the buying and selling of any other service and is thus morally good. They argue that we have a moral obligation to give the sex workers what they (supposedly) want—safe working conditions and moral approbation. Logically, moral praise ought to be extended to the customer and pimp, as well. What the redefinitional narrative fails to do, however, is provide any moral foundation for moral praise besides the fact of human agency. The fundamental assumption is that sexual libertinism is good for individuals and for all societies. To think otherwise is to deserve moral condemnation as "moralists" or "puritans." But it is not enough to simply insult one's opponents. How exactly does sexual libertinism benefit all people and cultures? Why ought commercial sex be morally acceptable? How does *this* cultural hegemony avoid the very criticisms of universalism it makes of other moral systems? People simply do not agree that everyone ought to do what is good in their own eyes. The philosophy of moral relativism, which undergirds sex worker advocacy, does not offer a way to justify its moral imperatives, and so the redefinitional salvation narrative simply becomes another universalist narrative among many. Sex worker advocates also exclude voices—for example, the voices of former prostitutes who have converted to Christianity and now see the sex trade for the evil that it is.

The commodification of sex promotes a body-mind dualism that is harmful to women. To view one's body as something that one uses and one can sell is to alienate oneself from one's own body. But because our bodies are an integral part of who we are, this dualistic attitude has the effect of de-meaning ourselves. It makes us less human when we buy and sell our bodies because we treat the human body as if it were a thing rather than a real person. Moreover, as feminist scholars have pointed out, dualism tends to promote the subjugation of women by associating them with the body—which is consistently less valued than the mind.[45] Legitimizing the sale of women's and children's bodies will do nothing to liberate them.

Do we really want a world where everything is for sale? Has the commodification of all aspects of life in our society been a blessing for us? Must everything have a price tag? Redefining prostitution as sex work is culturally imperialistic. It represents the globalization of consumerism taken to the uttermost. This has already occurred to an extent, of course—I've heard of a case where infants were being prostituted in Central America. If we already live in a world where men can buy sexual experiences with babies, we need to ask ourselves if legitimizing the purchase and sale of sexual intimacy is the right direction for our society and every society.

Sex worker advocates criticize anti-prostitution activists for hypocritically focusing on prostitution when other forms of labor are also abusive. This is not a fair criticism. De-meaning prostitutes is similar to other de-meaning forms of labor. The most obvious example is slavery—a system of labor that turns a human into property. Substantial and widespread anecdotal evidence indicates that many women and children are held in slavery as prostitutes. Moreover, the history of slavery in the United States (and elsewhere) certainly demonstrates the readiness of masters to sexually abuse or use their slaves. Sex tourism depends on master-slave fantasies of the relatively well-to-do Western tourist who will "sometimes rationalize their visits to the Caribbean for sex as a way to benefit the poor, oppressed women," while denying "exploitative aspects of their relationship."[46] But the modern anti-slavery movement, led by organizations such as *Not for Sale*, is not merely concerned with eliminating sexual slavery, but all forms

45. Noddings, *Women and Evil*, 26–27, 36.

46. Kempadoo, *Sexing the Caribbean*, 123–24.

of slavery. Nor does feminist or Christian concern for prostitutes preclude concern for labor exploitation, though any individual's or organization's efforts to help marginalized and exploited people are going to be limited by time and energy and focusing efforts on one group is not unreasonable.

Another key component of the redefinitional narrative is the idea that very few people are forced or tricked into the sex trade. Extensive anecdotal and statistical data indicate otherwise.[47] Moreover, many women really do feel like prostitution is their only viable option because of their poverty or other constricting circumstances. Yet advocates of sex worker "rights," accuse anti-prostitution activists of racism and neo-colonialism for their efforts to liberate women from the trade. Kempadoo, for example, describes feminist Kathleen Barry's work on trafficking as a "colonial . . . mission to rescue those whom she considered to be incapable of self-determination."[48] In fact, Kempadoo believes that anti-trafficking activists align with global capitalists when they describe prostitutes of developing nations "as incapable of making decisions about their own lives, forced by overwhelming external powers completely beyond their control into submission and slavery."[49] The irony of accusing feminist anti-trafficking scholars of being in bed with global capitalists while at the same time promoting a world where everything can be bought and sold seems lost on Kempadoo. More frightening, perhaps, is the denial of constricting forces on women's and children's lives that lead them to choose prostitution. Ultimately Kempadoo and others are

47. For example, see Brock and Thistlethwaite, *Casting Stones*; Clarke, "Prostitution for Everyone"; DeStefano, *The War on Human Trafficking*; Glenny, *McMafia*; McGill, *Human Traffic*; Farley et al., "Prostitution and Trafficking in Nine Countries"; Jewell, *Escaping the Devil's Bedroom*; Pulotu, "Prostitutes Talk of God"; Skinner, *A Crime So Monstrous*; Waugh, *Selling Olga*; United Nations Office on Drugs and Crime, *Global Report on Trafficking in Persons*; United States Department of State, *Trafficking in Persons Report*. My own personal conversations with prostitutes and former prostitutes in the developing world also support the contention that prostitution is a trap that harms women.

48. Kempadoo, "Introduction: Globalizing Sex Workers Rights," 11–12.

49. Ibid., 12.

suggesting that it is perfectly fine for poor women of color to be bought and sold, *and,* if one disagrees with this state of affairs, then one is a racist neo-colonialist!

Finally, sex worker advocates are unduly fascinated with the idea of "agency." Self-determination is, of course, a Western value held in high honor by the modern Western scholarly community. But recognition of marginalized people's autonomy ought not to obscure the forces that conspire to trap them in de-meaning circumstances. Everyone has choices, and everyone has social constraints. No one is perfectly free to define themselves independent of others. Critics of the anti-trafficking movement assume that if someone is a "victim," then she cannot have agency.[50] But this is a category error; one is a victim because one suffers de-meaning evil, not because one has lost agency. Those trying to help prostitutes leave the sex trade know that leaving the sex trade is a difficult personal choice precisely because of the social constraints these women face. Poverty, fear, the lack of an education, a history of sexual abuse, a drug or alcohol dependency, or poor coping skills do not negate a woman's agency, but they certainly do limit her freedom. When a woman continues to participate in her own self-destruction, she needs help in ending her participation, not encouragement in continuing it. Victims of abuse often need counseling to help them resist self-destructive responses; we should not confuse a coping mechanism—an attempt to resist de-meaning—with true freedom. Of course, we must listen to the women in the trade, and we need to respect their choices, but that is not the same as providing moral sanction for their acceptance of their defeat.

The language of rights is sometimes used to defend the concept of sex work. Certainly all people, including prostitutes, have both inherent rights—such as the right to the respect owed due to their infinite worth—and socially conferred rights—such as the right to police protection. Yet prostitutes do not have the "right" to engage in sex work. This is because work that is essentially de-meaning, both to the prostitute and to the consumer, runs counter to the inherent right to respect we share as humans loved by God.

50. See, for example, Sandy, "Just Choices," 195.

Those three women who posed before me in that brothel were daughters of God, beloved by God. Even for me to gaze on them as *things* would be disrespectful, de-meaning, and would violate their inherent human rights. Of course, police also need to respect prostitutes for the very same reasons I must, and this means taking seriously their obligation to protect them, even if prostitution is illegal. Moreover, abuse at the hands of police—such as demanding sex in lieu of paying a fine—is also a clear violation of human rights. Sex worker advocates are right to raise awareness of these and other human rights issues, but their case for the right to work as a prostitute cannot be sustained.

Certainly the redefinitional narrative is appealing to many people. It requires little of the average person while allowing the male consumer of sex to feel morally superior to all of the anti-sex puritan activists. Legitimizing sex work does not save anyone; rather, it consigns far too many women, children, and men to the dangers and degradations of prostitution. Prostitution is destructive to all involved—it turns intimate organs into commodities and people into things. Redefining prostitution will not change its fundamental de-meaning quality. It does not take evil seriously and offers little reason to oppose it. It will no doubt remain a popular narrative, but the women, men, and children trapped in prostitution deserve a better story.

The Christian gospel offers a better story. Evil is taken seriously—Christians do not need to deny the realities that conspire to trap people in prostitution, nor do they deny an individual's agency. In fact, Christians recognize that sometimes an individual's acts may promote their own self-destruction or the destruction of others. Rather than encouraging destructive acts to continue, Jesus invites sinners to "go and sin no more" (John 8:11). Moreover, Christians proclaim hope for a better life. Through the power of the Holy Spirit, people really may know happiness and experience healing (*re*-meaning), no matter what their present circumstances. The proof of the story is in the living—a faithful response to the invitation to enter into the life of Christ really does transform people and can heal them from horrendous evils. As I argued in the third chapter, this healing is a reality in the life of my friend Leslie and many other victims of evil. While a comprehensive soteriology is beyond the scope of this essay, I do wish to suggest four emphases that the sex trade reveals regarding our salvation story.

The first emphasis is on the need for rescue. No one likes to be rescued—we would rather be the rescuer. Being rescued does not deserve praise nor does it boost self-esteem. In fact, quite the opposite is true—*not* needing others is morally praiseworthy, at least in Western society. Advocates for sex workers make it quite clear that not every prostitute wants to be rescued, and they consider trying to rescue someone against their will to be morally blameworthy as well as ineffective. Yet, the Christian gospel teaches that our salvation is dependent upon God rescuing us. Though people are expected to participate in their own salvation, humanity is nonetheless entirely dependent upon the grace of God. The Psalms—the church's prayer book—teach an attitude of dependence to those who pray them. The prayer that Jesus taught his disciples is an excellent summary of the Psalms in this respect. In it, we ask God to reign over us, to give us our daily bread, to forgive us our sins, to keep us from trials and to deliver us from evil (Matt 6:9–13). The process of asking for these things teaches us the proper relation we have with God—that is, that we desperately need him and are wholly dependent upon him. Contrary to critical opinion, we do not seek to help others because it makes us feel good about ourselves, but because *we are being rescued too*, and we want to share the great gift we have discovered with others. In the clash with competing narratives, others might find comfort in refusing to think of themselves as needing God or others, but we nonetheless must live the good news that has been given to us: God loves us; we need God. What we discover as we live out this truth is that it works. God is faithful in keeping his promises.

But those who are part of the Christian mission to prostitutes be warned: viewing oneself as a "rescuer"—as someone who has a superior call—is spiritually dangerous to oneself and to those who are to be helped. Our participation in the Christian mission to prostitutes must be grounded in a self-understanding that acknowledges our *commonality* with prostitutes. We are all being rescued—if anyone is the rescuer, it is God, not us.

The second emphasis is on the power of God to transform lives. The secular academy is not lacking wisdom in its efforts to promote people's healing. To take one example, consider Judith Lewis Herman's *Trauma and Recovery*. Herman found parallels between the trauma incurred at the hands of domestic abuse and public political terror. She rightly taught that healing must occur in the context of relationships and follows three stages: safety, remembrance and mourning, and reconnection.[51] The Christian mission to prostitutes does well to mine the riches of this secular wisdom. But we also have something to offer that Herman and others do not have: a relationship with God who is able to save. Because we must own our salvation, our healing and recovery will not be magical or quick, but we can trust that God is for us and with us. We have always proclaimed and claimed the power of the resurrection for the healing of the world. Often and sometimes to our surprise, this power works concretely to heal people. The Gospels portray Christ as a healer, and the reign of God he announces is one where healing breaks through and transforms our lives. We have, perhaps, no greater practical wisdom than anyone else, but we do testify to the healing and transforming power of God in Christ at work in our lives, in our churches, and in the world.

Another emphasis of the salvation story that the sex trade reveals to us is the power of the gospel to overcome shame. In the modern West, we tend to favor a gospel of the forgiveness of sins over a gospel of honor for the shamed. But, of course, the gospel is both. Given the social ostracism felt by most prostitutes, as well as their frequent victimization, we do not need to make prostitutes feel bad. Proper guilt comes in time and forgiveness is near at hand, but what a prostitute needs is to be honored for the child of God he or she is. The Christian story has long held a different ethic of honor than the cultures it seeks to transform.[52] The

51. Herman, *Trauma and Recovery*, 133, 155.

52. See deSilva, *Honor, Patronage, Kinship & Purity*, especially chapters 1 and 2.

Christian mission to prostitutes needs to live this out by modeling how prostituted people can trade their shame in for honor within communities of grace. For this, we look to Jesus. Whenever anyone tried to shame Jesus, the shame was reflected back on to him, and when anyone sought his healing touch, their shame melted into honor.[53] By welcoming prostitutes into our churches and homes and valuing them for the people they are, we give them another message than the one they hear on the street. It is not enough for the missionaries to prostitutes to convey this message; the entire church needs to support it too. For too many Christians in the pews, a prostitute symbolizes sin and degradation. If we are to truly welcome and honor them—and thus promote their healing, then we need to see them as Jesus sees them: not as things, but as people, beloved by God.

Finally, I want to emphasize that prostitutes have a special place in the Christian story. Much of this comes from Judaism, where prostitutes like Rahab are portrayed as women of faith and Israel is sometimes symbolized as a prostitute who is nonetheless loved by God. The Gospels reinforce this emphasis by making specific mention of Jesus' ancestor Rahab and other shamed women (Matt 1:3, 5). "Loose women" are not turned away by Jesus, but rather are healed and blessed by him. In medieval church tradition, Mary the Magdalene was taken to be a prostitute, though there is little biblical evidence for it.[54] Similarly, the woman at the well who, according to John, becomes one of the first to proclaim the good news of the coming of Christ, has long been connected with the shame of sexual sin, though it does not seem that she was a prostitute (John 4:1–42). The church has cherished Jesus' mercy and kindness toward prostitutes and other shamed women and has a long tradition of using their stories as models of conversion and grace for the edification of the whole church.

53. See, for example, Luke 8:40–48. In effect, every healing and exorcism also removed shame.

54. She was a demoniac (Luke 8:2), which *might* imply prostitution. See Ward, *Harlots of the Desert*, 10–21. Ward believes she comes to represent unfaithfulness, and, through God's grace, a new Eve. But it was a short step from symbolic unfaithfulness to prostitute.

One of those stories involved Maria, the niece of Abraham, a monk of the desert. Maria had been left in the care of Abraham as a child, and he raised her to be a holy woman of God. But a wayward monk tempted her to give up her virginity. In guilt and shame, she forsook the desert and embraced prostitution. After some years, Abraham tracked her down and went to visit her, disguised as a soldier. When they were alone, he revealed himself to her and then pleaded for her salvation:

> After a while she plucked up courage and, weeping, she said to him, "I could not come to you; I was so very much ashamed. How can I pray again to God when I am defiled with sin which is as filthy as this?" The holy man said to her, "Upon me be your sin, Maria, and let God lay it to my account. Only listen to me and come, let us go back to where we belong. See, our dearest Ephraim is grieving so much for you and he is praying all the time for you to the Lord. My dear, do not draw back from the mercy of God. To you, your sins seem like mountains, but God has spread his mercy over all that He has made. So we once read together how an unclean woman came to the Lord and he did not send her away but cleansed her, and she washed his feet with her tears and wiped them with the hairs of her head. If sparks could set fire to the ocean, then indeed your sins could defile the purity of God! It is not new to fall, my daughter; what is wrong is to lie down when you have fallen."[55]

This plea becomes a plea for all of us. Are we really so different from Maria? Do we not all fall? Do we not all feel shame? See, the church is a church of prostitutes. We all need it to be a place of mercy, and that is why we must never forsake the mission to prostitutes.

In this chapter, I have sought to reflect briefly on how the problem of evil informs our ethical response to the sex trade. Evil is a practical problem of making sense of people's de-meaned lives. The sex trade exemplifies this process in all of its aspects: the sin, the shame, the slavery, the need for the mercy of God. The

55. Ward, *Harlots of the Desert*, 98.

Christian mission to prostitutes has critics who, in the end, want to keep the world much the way it already is. But we have a better story to tell: a story of grace, hope and healing. May we never tire of its telling.

* * *

I realize that to define evil as de-meaning is to define it in a very Christian way. Moreover, my claim that meaning must be relational and eternal is thoroughly Christian. Those readers that concur with this claim are likely Christians (or almost Christians) already. It is certainly possible to deny that evil is essentially de-meaning or that meaning must be relational and eternal, but I think that to do so impoverishes us and would lead ultimately to despair or indifference if we did not live better than we believe. In short, contrary to the arguments of atheists and others, I find the Christian response to evil to be deeply satisfying intellectually and emotionally. By this, I do not mean that faith in God is easy; in fact, my faith has cost me greatly.

This work represents more than a year of thought and reflection. Like some of my prayers, I have sometimes been startled by what I said. It may be that in my hesitant and stammering reply to the divine voice in my life I have not always spoken rightly about God, but God is my heart's desire, and so I trust in his grace to overlook and forgive any fault of mine. It seems most fitting to conclude with a prayer, both for myself and for all of those whose lives are threatened by horrendous evil:

> But may all who seek you rejoice and be glad in you;
>     may those who love your salvation say continually,
>         "Great is the Lord!"
> As for me, I am poor and needy,
>     but the Lord takes thought for me.
> You are my help and my deliverer;
>     do not delay, O my God.
>
> —Psalm 40:16–17 (NRSV)

# Works Cited


Abraham, William J. "Faraway Fields Are Green." In *God and the Philosophers: The Reconciliation of Faith and Reason*, edited by Thomas V. Morris, 162–72. Oxford: Oxford University Press, 1994.

Adams, Marilyn McCord. *Horrendous Evils and the Goodness of God*. Cornell Studies in the Philosophy of Religion. Ithaca: Cornell University Press, 1999.

Adler, Alfred. *The Science of Living*. London: Allen & Unwin, 1930.

Alston, William. "The Inductive Argument from Evil and the Human Cognitive Condition." In *The Evidential Argument from Evil*, edited by Daniel Howard-Snyder, 97–125. Bloomington: Indiana University Press, 1996.

Arendt, Hannah. *Eichmann in Jerusalem: A Report on the Banality of Evil*. Revised and enlarged edition. New York: Viking, 1964.

Azariah, V. S. "The Problem of Co-operation between Foreign and Native Workers." In *The History and Records of the Conference Together with Addresses Delivered at the Evening Meetings*, 306–15. Edinburg: Oliphant, Anderson & Ferrier; and New York: Revell, n.d. [1910]. https://archive.org/details/historyrecordsofooworliala (accessed 29 December 2015).

Bellatin, Mario. "Human Currency in Mexico's Drug Trade." Translated by Kurt Hollander. *The New York Times*. 27 March 2010. http://www.nytimes.com/2010/03/28/opinion/28bellatin.html (accessed 22 April 2010).

Bernstein, Elizabeth. *Temporarily Yours: Intimacy, Authenticity, and the Commerce of Sex*. Chicago: University of Chicago Press, 2007.

Brock, Rita Nakashima. *Journeys by Heart: A Christology of Erotic Power*. New York: Crossroad, 1988.

Brock, Rita Nakashima, and Rebecca Ann Parker. *Proverbs of Ashes: Violence, Redemptive Suffering and the Search for What Saves Us*. Boston: Beacon, 2001.

Brock, Rita Nakashima, and Susan Brooks Thistlethwaite. *Casting Stones: Prostitution and Liberation in Asia and the United States*. Minneapolis: Fortress, 1996.

Buber, Martin. *I and Thou*. 2nd ed. Translated by Ronald Gregor Smith. New York: MacMillan, 1958.

Camus, Albert. *The Plague*. Translated by Stuart Gilbert. New York: Random House, 1948.

Chapkis, Wendy. *Live Sex Acts: Women Performing Erotic Labor*. New York: Routledge, 1997.

Clarke, D. A. "Prostitution for Everyone: Feminism, Globalisation, and the 'Sex' Industry." In *Not for Sale: Feminists Resisting Prostitution and Pornography*, edited by Christine Stark and Rebecca Whisnant, 149–205. North Melbourne: Spinifex, 2004.

deSilva, David A. *Honor, Patronage, Kinship & Purity: Unlocking New Testament Culture*. Downers Grove, IL: InterVarsity, 2000.

DeStefano, Anthony M. *The War on Human Trafficking: U.S. Policy Assessed*. New Brunswick, NJ: Rutgers University Press, 2007.

Doezema, Jo. "Forced to Choose: Beyond the Voluntary v. Forced Prostitution Dichotomy." In *Global Sex Workers: Rights, Resistance, and Redefinition*, edited by Kamala Kempadoo and Jo Doezema, 34–47. New York: Routledge, 1998.

———. "International Activism: Interviews NWSP Coordinator, Cheryl Overs." In *Global Sex Workers: Rights, Resistance, and Redefinition*, edited by Kamala Kempadoo and Jo Doezema, 204–9. New York and London: Routledge, 1998.

———. "Ouch! Western Feminists' 'Wounded Attachment' to the 'Third World Prostitute.'" *Feminist Review* 67 (2001) 16–38.

Donovan, Josephine. *Feminist Theory: The Intellectual Traditions*. New York: Continuum, 2000.

Dostoyevsky, Fyodor. *The Brothers Karamazov*. Translated by Constance Garnett. Edited with a Foreword by Manuel Komroff. Signet Classic. New York: Signet, 1986.

Eire, Carlos. *A Very Brief History of Eternity*. Princeton: Princeton University Press, 2010.

Elshtain, Jean Bethke. *Augustine and the Limits of Politics*. Notre Dame: University of Notre Dame Press, 1998.

Emmons, Robert A. *The Psychology of Ultimate Concerns: Motivation and Spirituality in Personality*. New York: Guilford, 1999.

Farley, Melissa, et al. "Prostitution and Trafficking in Nine Countries: An Update on Violence and Posttraumatic Stress Disorder." In *Prostitution, Trafficking and Traumatic Stress*, edited by Melissa Farley, 33–74. Philadelphia: Haworth, 2003. http://www.prostitutionresearch.com/pdf/Prostitutionin9Countries.pdf (accessed 18 November 2015).

Fletcher, Richard. *The Barbarian Conversion: From Paganism to Christianity*. New York: Holt, 1998.

Friedman, Thomas L. *The World Is Flat: A Brief History of the Twenty-First Century*. Revised and expanded ed. New York: Farrar, Straus and Giroux, 2006.

Feuerbach, Ludwig. *The Essence of Christianity*. Translated from the 2nd German edition by Marian Evans. New York: Calvin Blanchard, 1855. http://books.google.com/books?id=Lsvo-mgtuc0C&dq (accessed 18 November 2015).

Gardiner, Judith Kegan. *Provoking Agents: Gender and Agency in Theory and Practice*. Urbana: University of Illinois Press, 1995.

Glenny, Misha. *McMafia: A Journey through the Global Criminal Underworld*. New York: Knopf, 2008.

Greenberg, Irving. "Cloud of Smoke, Pillar of Fire: Judaism, Christianity, and Modernity after the Holocaust." In *Auschwitz: Beginning of a New Era? Reflections on the Holocaust*, edited by Eva Fleischner, 7–55. New York: KTAV, 1977.

———. "Easing the Divine Suffering." In *The Life of Meaning: Reflections on Faith, Doubt, and Repairing the World*, edited by Bob Abernethy and William Bole, 67–74. New York: Seven Stories, 2007.

Gregory, Eric. *Politics and the Order of Love: An Augustinian Ethic of Democratic Citizenship*. Chicago: University of Chicago Press, 2008.

Hart, David Bentley. *The Doors of the Sea: Where Was God in the Tsunami?* Grand Rapids: Eerdmans, 2005.

Hasker, William. *The Triumph of God over Evil: Theodicy for a World of Suffering*. Strategic Initiatives in Evangelical Theology. Downers Grove, IL: InterVarsity, 2008.

Herman, Judith Lewis. *Trauma and Recovery*. New York: Basic, 1992.

Hume, David. "Evil and the God of Religion." In *The Problem of Evil: Selected Readings*, edited by Michael L. Peterson, 39–56. Library of Religious Philosophy. Notre Dame: University of Notre Dame Press, 1992.

Ilibagiza, Immaculée. *Left to Tell: Discovering God amidst the Rwandan Holocaust*. With Steve Erwin. Carlsbad, CA: Hay House, 2006.

Intelligence Squared, U.S. "It's Wrong to Pay for Sex." Transcript of televised debate. Moderator John Donovan. April 21, 2009. http://intelligencesquaredus.org/ index.php/past-debates/its-wrong-to-pay-for-sex/ (accessed 18 November 2015).

Islam, Jamal N. *The Ultimate Fate of the Universe*. Cambridge: Cambridge University Press, 2009.

Jeffreys, Sheila. "Prostitution as a Harmful Cultural Practice." In *Not for Sale: Feminists Resisting Prostitution and Pornography*, edited by Rebecca Whisnant and Christine Start, 386–99. North Melbourne: Spinifex, 2004.

Jenkins, Philip. *The New Faces of Christianity: Believing the Bible in the Global South*. Oxford: Oxford University Press, 2006.

———. *The Next Christendom: The Coming of Global Christianity*. Oxford: Oxford University Press, 2002.

Jewell, Dawn Herzog. *Escaping the Devil's Bedroom: Sex Trafficking, Global Prostitution and the Gospel's Transforming Power*. Foreword by Timothy C. Morgan. Oxford: Monarch, 2008.

Kelly, Joseph F. *The Problem of Evil in the Western Tradition: From the Book of Job to Modern Genetics*. Collegeville, MN: Liturgical, 2001.

Kempadoo, Kamala. "Introduction: Globalizing Sex Workers' Rights." In *Global Sex Workers: Rights, Resistance, and Redefinition*, edited by Kamala Kempadoo and Jo Doezema, 1–28. New York: Routledge, 1998.

———. *Sexing the Caribbean: Gender, Race, and Sexual Labor*. New York: Routledge, 2004.

Kimel, Alvin F., ed. *Speaking the Christian God: The Holy Trinity and the Challenge of Feminism*. Grand Rapids: Eerdmans, 1992.

Kwan, Kai-Man. "The Argument from Religious Experience." In *The Blackwell Companion to Natural Theology*, edited by William Lane Craig and J. P. Moreland, 498–552. Blackwell, 2009.

Koyama, Kosuke. *Waterbuffalo Theology*. Maryknoll, NY: Orbis, 1974.

LaCugna, Catherine Mowry. *God for Us: The Trinity and Christian Life*. San Francisco: HarperSanFrancisco, 1991.

Levenson, Jon D. *Resurrection and the Restoration of Israel: The Ultimate Victory of the God of Life*. New Haven: Yale University Press, 2006.

Lewis, C. S. *A Grief Observed*. Foreword by Madeleine L'Engle. San Francisco: HarperSanFrancisco, 1989.

———. *Mere Christianity*. A Revised and Enlarged Edition with a New Introduction. New York: Collier, 1960.

———. *The Problem of Pain*. New York: Macmillan, 1962.

Linville, Mark D. "The Moral Argument." In *The Blackwell Companion to Natural Theology*, edited by William Lane Craig and J. P. Moreland, 391–448. Malden, MA: Wiley-Blackwell, 2009.

Mackie, J. L. *Ethics: Inventing Right and Wrong*. New York: Penguin, 1977.

———. "Evil and Omnipotence." In *The Problem of Evil: Selected Readings*, edited by Michael L. Peterson, 89–101. Library of Religious Philosophy. Notre Dame: University of Notre Dame Press, 1992.

MacMullen, Ramsey. *Christianizing the Roman Empire (A.D. 100–400)*. New Haven: Yale University Press, 1984.

McGill, Craig. *Human Traffic: Sex, Slaves and Immigration*. London: Vision, 2003.

McGrew, Timothy, and Lydia McGrew. "The Argument from Miracles: A Cumulative Case for the Resurrection of Jesus of Nazareth." In *The Blackwell Companion to Natural Theology*, edited by William Lane Craig and J. P. Moreland, 593–662. Blackwell, 2009.

Montgomery, Heather. "Children, Prostitution, and Identity: A Case Study from a Tourist Resort in Thailand." In *Global Sex Workers: Rights, Resistance, and Redefinition*, edited by Kamala Kempadoo and Jo Doezema, 139–50. New York: Routledge, 1998.

Murray, Alison. "Debt-Bondage and Trafficking: Don't Believe the Hype." In *Global Sex Workers: Rights, Resistance, and Redefinition*, edited by Kamala Kempadoo and Jo Doezema, 51–64. New York: Routledge, 1998.

Neiman, Susan. *Evil in Modern Thought: An Alternative History of Philosophy*. With a New Preface by the Author. Princeton: Princeton University Press, 2002.

New Zealand Prostitution Law Review Committee. *Report of the Prostitution Law Review Committee on the Operation of the Prostitution Reform Act 2003*. Wellington: Ministry of Justice, 2008.

Nietzsche, Friedrich. *On the Genealogy of Morals*. In *Basic Writings of Nietzsche*, translated and edited with commentaries by Walter Kaufmann, 437–599. New York: Modern Library, 1992.

———. "Skirmishes of an Untimely Man." In *Twilight of the Idols or, How One Philosophizes with a Hammer*. In *The Portable Nietzsche*, edited and translated by Walter Kaufmann, 513–56. New York: Penguin, 1976.

———. "The 'Improvers' of Mankind." In *Twilight of the Idols or, How One Philosophizes with a Hammer*. In *The Portable Nietzsche*, edited and translated by Walter Kaufmann, 501–5. New York: Penguin, 1976.

———. "Why I Am a Destiny." In *Ecce Homo*. In *Basic Writings of Nietzsche*, translated and edited with commentaries by Walter Kaufmann, 782–91. New York: Modern Library, 1992.

Noddings, Nel. *Women and Evil*. Berkeley: University of California Press, 1989.

O'Neil, Shannon. "The Real War in Mexico: How Democracy Can Defeat the Drug Cartels." *Foreign Affairs* 88 (2009) 63–77.

Owens-Bullard, Becky. "Take off the cape: Why using the word 'rescue' is harmful to anti-trafficking efforts." *Colorado Coalition against Sexual Assault Blog*, 24 July 2014. http://www.ccasa.org/take-off-the-cape/ (accessed 18 November 2015).

Parker, Joe. "How Prostitution Works." In *Not for Sale: Feminists Resisting Prostitution and Pornography*, edited by Christine Stark and Rebecca Whisnant, 3–14. North Melbourne: Spinifex, 2004.

Parker, Theodore. "Of Justice and the Conscience." In *Ten Sermons of Religion*, 66–101. 2nd ed. Boston: Ticknor & Fields, 1861.

Patrick, Saint. *The Confession of St. Patrick and Letter to Coroticus*. Translated by John Skinner. Foreword by John O'Donohue. New York: Doubleday, 1998.

Peterson, Michael L. *The Problem of Evil: Selected Readings*. Notre Dame: University of Notre Dame Press, 1992.

Plantinga, Alvin. "The Free Will Defense." In *The Problem of Evil: Selected Readings*, edited by Michael L. Peterson, 103–33. Library of Religious Philosophy. Notre Dame: University of Notre Dame Press, 1992.

Pocock, Michael, Gailyn Van Rheenen, and Douglas McConnell. *The Changing Face of World Missions: Engaging Contemporary Issues and Trends*. Grand Rapids: Baker Academic, 2005.

Pulotu, Soane Malia. "Prostitutes Talk of God." *Melanesian Journal of Theology* 21, no. 1 (2005) 84–91.

Porterfield, Amanda. *Healing in the History of Christianity*. Oxford: Oxford University Press, 2005.

Raymond, Janice G., et al. *A Comparative Study of Women Trafficked in the Migration Process: Patterns, Profiles and Health Consequences of Sexual Exploitation in Five Countries (Indonesia, the Philippines, Thailand, Venezuela and the United States)*. Coalition Against Trafficking in Women, 2002. http://action.web.ca/home/catw/readingroom.shtml?x=17062 (accessed 18 November 2015).

Robinson, John A. T. *Can We Trust the New Testament?* Grand Rapids: Eerdmans, 1977.

Rogoziński, Jan. *A Brief History of the Caribbean: From the Arawak and Carib to the Present*. Rev. ed. New York: Penguin Putnam, 2000.

Rowe, William L. "Friendly Atheism, Skeptical Theism, and the Problem of Evil." *International Journal for Philosophy of Religion* 59 (2006) 79–92.

———. "The Problem of Evil and Some Varieties of Atheism." *American Philosophical Quarterly* 16, no. 4 (1979) 335–41.

Ruffins, Ebonne. "Rescuing Girls from Sex Slavery." *CNN Heroes*. 30 April 2010. http://www.cnn.com/2010/LIVING/04/29/cnnheroes.koirala.nepal/ (accessed 18 November 2015).

Russell, Bertrand. "Education." In *The Basic Writings of Bertrand Russell, 1903–1959*, 401–12. London: Routledge, 1992.

———. "A Free Man's Worship." In *Mysticism and Logic and Other Essays*, 40–47. Totowa, NJ: Barnes & Noble, 1981.

———. "Individual and Social Ethics." In *The Basic Writings of Bertrand Russell, 1903–1959*, 357–66. London: Routledge, 1992.

———. *My Philosophical Development*. Rev. ed. London: Routledge, 1995.

———. "The Social Responsibilities of Scientists." In *Fact and Fiction*, 228–31. London: Routledge, 1994.

———. "What I Believe." In *The Basic Writings of Bertrand Russell, 1903–1959*, 367–90. London: Routledge, 1992.

———. "Why I Am Not a Communist." In *The Basic Writings of Bertrand Russell, 1903–1959*, 479–84. London: Routledge, 1992.

Sandy, Larissa. "Just Choices: Representations of Choice and Coercion in Sex Work in Cambodia." *Australian Journal of Anthropology* 18, no. 2 (2007) 194–206.

Schumm, Darla Y. "The Self-Understanding of the Christian Missionary Movement on Prostitution in Thailand: A Critical Analysis." PhD diss., Vanderbilt University, 2002.

Singer, Jefferson A., and Peter Salovey. *The Remembered Self: Emotion and Memory in Personality*. New York: Free, 1993.

Skinner, E. Benjamin. *A Crime So Monstrous: Face-to-Face with Modern-Day Slavery*. New York: Free, 2008.

Styron, William. *Sophie's Choice: A Novel*. New York: Random House, 1979.

Stump, Eleonore. "Faith and the Problem of Evil." In *Seeking Understanding: The Stob Lectures, 1986–1998*, 491–550. Grand Rapids: Eerdmans, 2001.

———. *Wandering in Darkness: Narrative and the Problem of Suffering*. Oxford: Clarendon, 2010.

Surin, Kenneth. *Theology and the Problem of Evil*. Signposts in Theology. Oxford: Blackwell, 1986.

Swinburne, Richard. *Providence and the Problem of Evil*. Oxford: Oxford University Press, 1998.

Thielicke, Helmut. *A Little Exercise for Young Theologians*. Introduction by Martin E. Marty. Translated by Charles L. Taylor. Grand Rapids: Eerdmans, 1962.

Unamuno, Miguel de. *Tragic Sense of Life*. Translated by J. E. Crawford Flitch. New York: Dover, 1954.

United Nations Office on Drugs and Crime. *Global Report on Trafficking in Persons*. February 2009. http://www.unodc.org/unodc/en/human-trafficking/global-report-on-trafficking-in-persons.html (accessed 18 November 2015).

United States Department of State. *Trafficking in Persons Report*. June 2009. http://www.state.gov/j/tip/rls/tiprpt/2009/index.htm (accessed 18 November 2015).

Volf, Miroslav. *Free of Charge: Giving and Forgiving in a Culture Stripped of Grace*. Grand Rapids: Zondervan, 2005.

Walls, Jerry L. "Outrageous Evil and the Hope of Healing: Our Practical Options." In *Immersed in the Life of God: The Healing Resources of the Christian Faith: Essays in Honor of William J. Abraham*, 186–201. Grand Rapids: Eerdmans, 2008.

Ward, Benedicta. *Harlots of the Desert: A Study of Repentance in Early Monastic Sources*. Cistercian Studies Series 106. Kalamazoo, MI: Cistercian, 1987.

Watson, Natalie K. *Feminist Theology*. Guides to Theology. Grand Rapids: Eerdmans, 2003.

Waugh, Louisa. *Selling Olga: Stories of Human Trafficking and Resistance*. London: Phoenix, 2006.

Weitzer, Ronald. "The Movement to Criminalize Sex Work in the United States." *Journal of Law and Society* 37, no. 1 (2010) 61–84.

Wolterstorff, Nicholas. *Lament for a Son*. Grand Rapids: Eerdmans, 1987.

Wykstra, Stephen. "The Humean Obstacle to Evidential Arguments from Suffering: On Avoiding the Evils of 'Appearance.'" *International Journal for the Philosophy of Religion* 16 (1984) 73–94.

Yancey, Philip. *What's So Amazing about Grace?* Grand Rapids: Zondervan, 1997.

Printed in Great Britain
by Amazon